Unbought Spirit

John Jay Chapman, ca. 1915.
(Courtesy of the Century Association.)

Unbought Spirit

A John Jay Chapman Reader

Edited by Richard Stone

Foreword by Jacques Barzun

University of Illinois Press
Urbana and Chicago

© 1998 by the Board of Trustees of the University of Illinois
Foreword © 1998 by Jacques Barzun
Manufactured in the United States of America
1 2 3 4 5 C P 5 4 3 2 1
This book is printed on acid-free paper.

Library of Congress Cataloging-in-Publication Data
Chapman, John Jay, 1862–1933.
Unbought spirit : a John Jay Chapman reader /
edited by Richard Stone ; foreword by Jacques Barzun.
   p.   cm.
Includes bibliographical references (p.   ).
ISBN 0-252-02417-6 (acid-free paper)
ISBN 0-252-06724-X (pbk. : acid-free paper)
I. Stone, Richard, 1953– II. Title.
PS1292.C3 A6   1998
814'.52—ddc21   98-8929
CIP

He had the obstinate pride, the incorruptibility of a being who should propose to be the *first man,—* the one unbought spirit in the universe.

—John Jay Chapman on Alfred Q. Collins, *Memories and Milestones*

Contents

Foreword by *Jacques Barzun* ix
Introduction xiii
Editor's Note xxiii
Acknowledgments xxv

Selections from John Jay Chapman's Works
  Coatesville 1
  Politics 5
  Between Elections 14
  The Unity of Human Nature 25
  The Doctrine of Non-Resistance 35
  William James 43
  Dr. Horace Howard Furness 49
  Julia Ward Howe 57
  Maria Weston Chapman 64
  Learning 72
  The Function of a University 93

Professorial Ethics *98*
Greek as a Pleasure *106*
Emerson *112*
Robert Browning *172*
Unpublished Correspondence *189*

Bibliography *207*

Foreword

JACQUES BARZUN

In the essay introducing one of his plays, George Bernard Shaw bursts out impatiently at his contemporaries for being deaf and blind to the genius of Samuel Butler. I feel the same way about the Americans of my time as regards John Jay Chapman. But unlike Shaw, I am far from having been the only voice proclaiming Chapman's genius. William James in *The Varieties of Religious Experience* called him "a profound moralist." That was during Chapman's lifetime. A decade or more after his death, Edmund Wilson pointed out in detail what a superb literary and cultural critic Chapman was. Meanwhile, M. A. DeWolfe Howe, by editing a selection of Chapman's correspondence, had demonstrated that here was one of the few great American letter writers.

That should be enough for fame. But there is more to be said. Anybody who reads Chapman's political writings—notably *Practical Agitation*—can see that as an observer of democracy at work, Chapman rivals Henry Adams and Brooks Adams in his analysis and surpasses them in the vividness of his direct experience. Finally, as I argued in offering an earlier anthology of Chapman writings in 1957, the deed at Coatesville after the lynching there of a black man makes Chapman *the* pioneer of our era of civil rights, his place in it not merely that of activist but of hero.

Now, how to account for his stubborn obscurity? One reason surely is the range of his powers. More perhaps than elsewhere, a genius in America must specialize, that is, repeat himself. Then, slowly, his name is associated with some one thing that rings a bell: Melville? Ah, yes. Let me see—ships, in fact, whales! We profess to admire the type called Renaissance Man, but in practice we never seem to get beyond naming one, Leonardo da Vinci. We enjoy the surprise that he was a great painter and an engineer to boot. It flatters our sense of what really matters that he built bridges and designed a flying machine. It could not fly, but never mind, his genius was in the right place.

We have forgotten that the true Renaissance Man is the one whose mind is immersed creatively not only in practical doings and fine art but also in all that pertains to the highest human interests, from morals and religion to the political state and social rights, and thence to the study of the individual self in life and literature. In the roster of those who have been explorers on this scale, John Jay Chapman must be counted, despite his relatively small output. The samples of his work in this volume will show how much breadth and variety of perception can be concentrated in brief compass.

There is, to be sure, another obstacle to his easy acceptance: he is a stunningly lucid writer. Given the innate pedantry of the modern mind, this hurdle is hard to get over. When we see what contemporary readers choose to turn into worldwide best-sellers, we begin to make out what it takes to captivate the great public. First, you must write a very long book, offer it as a novel, but make your characters deliver harangues on theological points, complete with sentences in Latin (untranslated), which in these United States not one person in ten million can understand. It's safe also to discuss Arabic sources of Western thought, to sprinkle the text with obscure allusions, and in general bring what is supposed to be a thriller down to traffic-jam pace. Critical praise and word-of-mouth advertising will persuade the many that they are taking part in an elevated ritual sure to confer virtue.

The ability to write such a work is not given to every talent. So in presenting John Jay Chapman, I must appeal to a still higher snobbery. I have admitted his drawback: he is as clear as a bright day; hence in reading him one cannot simply scan the words with a fluctuating awareness of their drift, confident that a useful mental residue accumulates while time passes. Instead, one must think and also feel, without letup, the reality that the words were meant to reproduce.

As in the first swim of the season, taking the plunge is the hard part. After that, the medium soon feels warm and friendly, healthful, invigorating, and at the end one comes out in a state that must be called nothing less than exhilaration. Do not mistake me: the chilling plunge is not into abstruse ideas. What Chapman writes about is what you find discussed in today's *New York Times* and *Wall Street Journal*, in the *New York Review of Books*, the *Economist*, and the *Times Literary Supplement*.

The subscribers to these journals in this country seem to me intended by providence to be Chapman readers. They are presumably men and women to whom attaining the B.A. has not served as a rampart against the force of original thought, the appeal of style, the electric shock of wit, the enveloping movement of deep feeling—in short, they have not abandoned serious reading at the word *Commencement*.

It is for these happy few—and may they turn out numerous in an absolute sense—that Richard Stone has made his choice of Chapman pieces, a choice as judicious as it is lavish. He is to be praised twice over for his initiative; it will give lasting pleasure to the individual partaker and it will once more alert the professional literary or cultural historian to the fact that Chapman is a missing figure in the American pantheon. That ideal building is not so crowded that the nation can afford to keep overlooking a candidate of his stature.

Introduction

John Jay Chapman was a tall man who in middle life and old age wore a rich, full beard—a beard that suggested to many the prophets of Israel. He had piercing, brilliant, small eyes; and, according to his first biographer, M. A. DeWolfe Howe, he was elaborately scarved in all weathers.

The story behind Chapman's loss of his left hand throws into relief the passionate nature of the man. In his midtwenties, while courting his first wife, he mistakenly believed that Percival Lowell had designs on Minna Timmins. He thrashed the astronomer (and future discoverer of Pluto) with a heavy cane. As an act of penance, after finding that his suspicions were unjust and mistaken, he thrust his left hand into a coal fire and kept it there till the hand was effectively destroyed.

Chapman wrote twenty-five books on varied subjects. He wrote plays and translations of the classics. He wrote about figures as diverse as Balzac, Browning, Dante, Euripides, Kipling, Shakespeare, and Shaw. What Chapman says of Shakespeare is also true of himself: he had a fully integrated mind. As Melvin Bernstein has observed, we do not find compartmentalization in Chapman—his brain is not divided into sections, one that composes religious meditations, another that analyzes and criticizes literature, and yet another that produces social criticism. He was deliberately and emphatically antispecialist. His books and uncollected writings constitute an embrace of the world at large. He criticized the ancients in *Greek Genius and Other Essays* (1915) and *Lucian, Plato, and Greek Morals* (1931); summarized the legacy of William Lloyd Garrison (1913); attacked big business (*Causes and Consequences*, 1898) and the commercialization of education (*Learning and Other Essays*, 1910); apotheosized religious emotion in *Letters and Religion* (1924); and wrote on diverse subjects for Frank Crowninshield's *Vanity Fair* between 1918 and 1925. Allusiveness and a broad range of reference distinguish Chapman's work, early and late. His mind is a unity in which things are cognate, in which one aspect comments upon another.

In his searching study of 1937, Edmund Wilson lamented: "At the present time hardly one reader in a million has heard of even the name of John Jay Chapman. His later books had no circulation, and most of his earlier ones are out of print" ("John Jay Chapman," *Triple Thinkers* 133). So it remains. Not admitted to the constellation of American thinkers that now includes his friend William James and his acquaintance Henry Adams, Chapman continues to attract only a small band of admirers. This anthology is born of the conviction that Chapman is one of our contemporaries. Chapman warned of compromise and scientism, of the seductions of authority and the classifying and specializing intellect, of the impulse to despair. He wrote, in other words, of the news that stays news. He is a tonic to cynicism and an antidote to a society gone flaccid and complacent.

To read Chapman is to feel his force and power; to read him is to open a door and release a coursing draught of idealism and wit. When we pick up one of Chapman's books, we do not enter a labyrinth or maze in which we need guide books to thread our way. We do not find ourselves adrift in a sea of lore and recondite allusion. In this, he is very unlike those exemplars of difficulty, Dante and Joyce—he does not encourage elucidation and exegesis. Like William Hazlitt, Chapman is an original; he does not derive from anyone but himself. Wilson is enlightening on this theme: "Perhaps our most vivid impression as we read about Chapman in M.A. DeWolfe Howe's [*John Jay Chapman and His Letters*]—especially through the first half of his life—is that we have encountered a personality who does not belong in his time and place and who by contrast makes us aware of the commonness, the provinciality, and the timidity of most of his contemporaries" ("John Jay Chapman," *Triple Thinkers* 134).

It is instinct for Chapman to cut to the bone, to try to get to the heart of things and expose, without obfuscation and formal manners, the essence of his subject. He must always articulate his experience in an unfussy way.

It was in such fashion that he made his debut on the literary scene. When Chapman's *Emerson and Other Essays* appeared in 1898, its author had already seen some of his work in print. His first separate publication, the slight *The Two Philosophers* of 1892, was a satire on a philosophical dispute between Professors Josiah Royce and F. E. Abbot of Harvard. It was preceded by Chapman's commentary and terza rima rendering of Dante's "The Fourth Canto of the Inferno," which first appeared in the *Atlantic Monthly* in 1890 and was included in Chapman's *Dante* of 1927. In 1898, Chapman was one year into his four-year stewardship of the *Political Nursery*, an iconoclastic political and literary monthly that featured commentary on local, national, and international affairs. But it is with his book on Emerson and particularly the title essay that Chapman announced his presence. Here Chapman is his characteristically unfettered, and unsublimated, self. Although ostensibly belles lettres, this book is as much about American society as it is about literature.

As Richard Hovey has suggested, Chapman's essay on Browning is a kind of companion to the one on Emerson. It too opens with an apostrophe or paean to its subject's virtues. Browning, Chapman tells us, is robust, vital, whole, a genuinely religious person. Chapman says that Browning believes in the individual soul. "The first two fundamental beliefs of Browning—namely:

(1) that, ultimately speaking, the most important matter in the world is the soul of a man; and (2) that a sense of effort is coincident with development—are probably true." Browning is at odds with conventional morality because it submerges the individual.

In *Causes and Consequences* (1898) and *Practical Agitation* (1900), Chapman's concern with the degradation of society and the individual becomes overt along with his sustaining belief in unselfishness. In his reading of history, the close of the Civil War brought on an era in which commerce held sway over all things and sealed minds, hearts, and lips. The railroads that crisscrossed the country had become vehicles and conduits of greed. The railroads made corruption easy, convenient, and profitable. In the first book, Chapman argues that "a civilization based upon a commerce which is in all its parts corruptly managed will present a social life which is unintelligent and mediocre, made up of people afraid of each other, whose ideas are shopworn, whose manners are self-conscious" (64). Here, the prescient Chapman gazes into his glass and predicts the depersonalization of twentieth-century society.

Still, Chapman is neither nihilist nor pessimist. In fact, his books glow with meliorism. Yes, they seem to be saying, evils are terribly visible, a lack of faith is pervasive and enervating and failure common; corruption and compromise are rampant. But healing goes on inexorably, inevitably. It could not be otherwise. For Chapman, the democratic institutions in America reveal the natures of people. We find "in democracy a frame of government by which private selfishness, the bane and terror of all government, is thrust brutally to the front and kept there, staring in hideous openness" (*Causes* 130–31). Chapman looks into the abyss without averting his gaze and without flinching and then makes his way back to hope.

In 1901, the year following the publication of *Practical Agitation*, Chapman collapsed while giving a speech in a small town near Philadelphia. Thus began the breakdown that would cleave his life in two. After his collapse, he made his way to New York

City and from there to Rokeby, the estate of his wife's family, in Barrytown, New York. There he lay in a darkened room. In "Retrospections," his unfinished autobiography, Chapman relates that he felt like the man in *The Pit and the Pendulum:* "I must lie perfectly still while the circular saw or swinging scythe filed the core of me. If I resisted I destroyed myself. Some of those midnights were unforgettable. In the early morning the dim light that came in a slit above the roller shade smote me like a mace and waked me to pain" (M. A. DeWolfe Howe 153–54). Chapman spent a year in bed, during which time he had to be bathed, fed, and dressed. He lost the ability to walk and had to rely on crutches. The beauty of a Catskill Mountain sunset and the splendor of an Italian church would soon oppress him and prove too much for his shattered nerves. He spent two winters in Edgewater, a place belonging to his wife, where he gathered strength. There he studied musical harmony and cultivated the society of the local inhabitants. When Mrs. Chapman asked him what he talked about with one or two of them, he replied that they do not talk—that he keeps "wondering whether the black things in his beard are melon-seeds or cockroaches" (M. A. DeWolfe Howe 157). For no matter how oppressive external circumstance or inward pressure might be, Chapman never lost his fascination with the human comedy or his delight in the vagaries of human nature, which run like a leitmotif through his life and letters. High spirits and gravity of thought coexist, not clash, in Chapman.

In 1905 Chapman established himself in Sylvania, a majestic house built by his friend Charles Platt on a tract of land adjoining Edgewater and Rokeby. Chapman became productive again in 1908, when he began publishing plays for adults and children. He and his wife ran a settlement house in Manhattan that year as well.

Chapman's mysterious and appalling illness did not and could not break him from his habits of engagement. The first piece of cultural criticism since his breakdown and the first of many salvos Chapman would fire at his alma mater is "The Harvard

Classics and Harvard." In the example of his old school giving its name to Collier's "five-foot shelf" of classics, Chapman saw commerce and education tie an incestuous knot. For Chapman, "the men who control Harvard to-day are very little else than business men, running a large department store which dispenses education to the million. Their endeavor is to make it the *largest* establishment of the kind in America.... In devising new means of expansion, new cash registers, new stub systems and credit systems—systems for increasing their capital and the volume of their trade—these business men have unconsciously (and I think consciously also) adopted any method that would give results. A few years ago their attention was focused upon increasing their capital (new buildings and endowment): to-day it is focused upon increasing their trade (numbers of students)" ("Harvard Classics" 440).

Chapman always wrote about things under his skin. He looked at higher education through the prism of Harvard because he had known the school intimately since getting his baccalaureate and law degrees in the 1880s. He kept up with developments through correspondence and frequent visits, especially after his sons Conrad, Victor, and Chanler matriculated. He knew Royce and James, Kittredge and Francis Child, and Charles Eliot Norton and President Eliot. In his quarrels with Harvard, Chapman's capacity for righteous indignation and his sense of humor stood him in good stead.

No man whose life was stamped by so much activity and dramatic intensity could ever turn into a passive bystander. Involved in a personal way with the tumultuous events of World War I, he first agitated on behalf of compulsory disarmament but through most of it fulminated against German propaganda and American timidity. His 1914 book *Deutschland über Alles* dissects political thought in Germany. The death in 1916 of his son Victor, an aviator for the Lafayette Escadrille, made Chapman supersensitive to criticism of the Allies. Chapman responded like a tuning fork to the vacillating policies of Woodrow Wilson. He also began a crusade against the influence of the Roman

Catholic church, which, he believed, tried to control education in America and subvert free speech and independent expression. The earliest statement of Chapman's antipapism is "The Roman Church" from *Notes on Religion*. The first part of that 1915 essay formulates a classic Protestant response to the danger and tyranny of dogma. *The Spiritual Guide of Molinos*, published in 1675, "contained two ideas, each of which Molinos believed in with an absolute faith, and which was nevertheless in the last analysis destructive of one another. The first idea was the idea of the direct union of the soul with God,—a union so close as to make a priesthood unnecessary,—the second was the idea of the authority of the church" (13). He goes on to say, "The idea is that a thing can both be and not be. The good Catholic believes his soul to be in direct union with God. And yet the church is between them. The two ideas of Molinos' contradict one another" (14). The second part of that essay develops Chapman's perception of the church in America as a dangerous, powerful, and seductive influence.

In Chapman's thinking, Christ is the supreme practical agitator and Christianity the natural and inevitable expression of his vision. "Christ was able to hold a prism perfectly still in his hand so as to dissolve a ray of light into its elements. Every time he speaks, he splits open humanity, as a man might crack a nut and show the kernel. The force of human feeling behind these sayings can be measured only by their accomplishments. They have been re-arranging and overturning human society ever since. By this most unlikely means of quiet demonstration in word and deed, did he unlock this gigantic power. The bare fragments of his talk open the sluices of our minds; they overwhelm and re-create. That was his method. The truth which he conveyed with such metaphysical accuracy lives now in the living. Very likely we cannot express it in dogmas, for such intellect as it takes to utter a dogma is not in us. But we need have no fear for our power of expressing it. It is enough for us to see truth; for if we see it, everything we do will express it" ("The Doctrine of Non-Resistance," *Learning and Other Essays* 204). It is not surprising to find in Chapman a resolutely Western mysticism: "The East is more interested in ideas than in conduct. But Christ's words pass into the practical part of men" (*Letters and Religion* 73).

The criticism that Chapman wrote after 1910 is as pungent as his earlier work. There is an excellent piece on Balzac in *Greek Genius* and a very provocative book on Shakespeare (the focus of which is on the proper performance of the plays rather than the more predictable thematic questions). There are fluent, readable translations (among them, *Homeric Scenes, Two Greek Plays, The Antigone of Sophocles*). In Edmund Wilson's view, Chapman "perfects himself now as a writer: in these books, the 'style all splinters,' of which William James wrote at the time of *Practical Agitation,* is hammered out into an instrument of perfect felicity, economy, limpidity, precision and point" ("John Jay Chapman," *Triple Thinkers* 156). The fierceness of the man is finally tempered. In the two decades before his death in 1933 at the age of seventy-one, Chapman wrote like an American Proust about the social and intellectual world of the privileged class to which he belonged. There are moving memorials of Isabella Stewart Gardner, Thomas Mott Osborne, H. H. Furness, Alfred Q. Collins, Charles Eliot, Charles Eliot Norton, and William James. Richard Hovey has noted that the eulogy is a new genre for him, a new vein to mine. Like his other writings, these pieces are not formally structured but are ruminative. These transcriptions of opinions, memories, experiences are ordered by the flow in which they enter Chapman's mind—they are not stream of consciousness, not automatic writing, but still they correspond to the ebb and flow of perception. More than anything else they are familiar essays.

His accomplishments notwithstanding, readers may still not be able to give Chapman their full approbation. It is not easy to make peace with him, for he is so unsettling. There is the matter of the man's perpetual cross-grainedness—a cross-grainedness that is going to offend every reader sooner or later. In particular, his crusade against the Roman Catholic church in the 1920s and the anti-Semitic statements he made during these years are bound to alienate. On occasion the prophet in Chapman can still subdue the nativist. The champion of Zola and Dreyfus and celebrant of the Hebrew Bible showed all of his earlier self in a 1920 memorial essay for Isaac Klein, his ally and partner in municipal reform. Chapman wrote in opposition to Prohibition and lashed out at Harvard in 1923 for segregating black students in the freshman dormitories. These are liberal eddies in what is now a fairly reactionary stream. The unitary beauty of Chapman's politics before World War I is gone.

Doubtless the vitriolic pen of the born polemicist and master controversialist sometimes makes it hard to see the lamb within the lion. The ideals of abolition help us see the man whole and entire. Chapman's book on William Lloyd Garrison has a special vitality because Chapman grew up with a psychological bond to his subject.

In terms of fact, Chapman did not know Garrison. Garrison was his grandmother's antislavery colleague. But John Jay Chapman cut his teeth on Maria Weston Chapman's remembrances of Garrison's courage and fundamental simplicity. A hatred of slavery and its aftereffects was bred in his bones.

Chapman did justice to his grandmother's legacy a half century after the Civil War. On 12 August 1911, a black man by the name of Zachariah Walker was lynched in Coatesville, Pennsylvania. When Walker was caught in the act of holding up a foreigner near a foundry, he shot and killed a security officer of the Worth Brothers Steel Company. He then ran up a tree, shot himself in the mouth, fell to the ground, and was taken to the hospital, from which he was removed along with the cot on which he lay. Then both were burned. Walker was thrown into the flames three times and his charred remains became playthings for children. No one in town admitted responsibility, but thousands watched the gruesome event.

Chapman brooded about the meaning of Coatesville for a year and then returned on the anniversary of the lynching to hold a prayer meeting and to do penance for all America. He expected a crowd at the meeting, but only three people showed up—a stool pigeon, an elderly black woman, and Edith Martin, a faith healer friend from New York who followed Chapman westward. Chapman nevertheless made his speech. He had no interest in becoming famous. The Coatesville occurrence epitomizes Chapman's fate, in every sense. Chapman conceived of the abolitionist era as "a great possession of the American people—if they ever come into their possessions" (M. A. DeWolfe Howe 268). So it must be with Chapman and Coatesville. In the Coatesville address, Chapman offers a vision of the American soul in bondage to the meaning of slavery. He writes of a people under the dominion of cruelty and killing. The coiled serpent of hate is his real subject. But that is only a part of his vision, for he also offers a glimpse of the love that is the only way out of that living death.

What he said and did at Coatesville opens a doorway into the house of Chapman. Coatesville gives his life its essential shape, proportion, and perspective; it summarizes and completes all that he set out to do. Round about the Coatesville address hang his other words, his other deeds. It is time at last to pay heed to this critic, moralist, and writer; time to let the goad that is Chapman do its work; but most of all it is time to let John Jay Chapman have his say.

Editor's Note

The date at the close of each essay indicates the year of first publication. Some of the essays were prepared with periodicals in mind while others were written as chapters of books. There is overlap in the case of magazine articles that Chapman reprinted in his volumes of miscellany. The following citations provide the publishing history of each essay. At least two essays appeared in obscure journals in addition to those cited here, but these are not listed because this is a book for the general reader, not the specialist.

M. A. DeWolfe Howe transcribed correspondence he was unable to print in *John Jay Chapman and His Letters*. The letters published here follow Howe's versions, which were deposited at the Houghton Library. It should be noted that I have silently corrected a very small number of obvious typos. In every other way this edition preserves John Jay Chapman's habits and practices of style and punctuation. Chapman's method of capitalizing words for emphasis in one place and not another is orthographical evidence of a nature formed by the nineteenth century.

"Coatesville" was published in *Harper's Weekly*, 21 September 1912, and reprinted in the collection *Memories and Milestones* in 1915.

"Politics" is the first third of "The Capture of Government by Commercialism" published in *Atlantic Monthly*, February 1898, and reprinted as a chapter of *Causes and Consequences* in 1898.

"Between Elections" is the first half of "Between Elections" published in *Atlantic Monthly*, January 1900, and reprinted as a chapter of *Practical Agitation* in 1900.

"The Unity of Human Nature" was published in *Learning and Other Essays* in 1910.

"The Doctrine of Non-Resistance" was published in *Political Nursery*, December 1900, and reprinted in *Learning and Other Essays* in 1910.

"William James" was published in *Harvard Graduates' Magazine*, December 1910, and reprinted in *Memories and Milestones* in 1915.

"Dr. Horace Howard Furness" was published in *Harper's Weekly*, 23 November 1912, and reprinted in *Memories and Milestones* in 1915.

"Julia Ward Howe" was published in *Memories and Milestones* in 1915.

"Maria Weston Chapman" was published in *Atlantic Monthly*, May 1914, and reprinted in *Memories and Milestones* in 1915.

"Learning" was published in *Atlantic Monthly*, July 1910, and reprinted in *Learning and Other Essays* in 1910.

"The Function of a University" was published in *Political Nursery*, August 1900.

"Professorial Ethics" was published in *Science*, 1 July 1910, and reprinted in *Learning and Other Essays* in 1910.

"Greek as a Pleasure" was published in *Boston Evening Transcript*, 17 September 1913, and reprinted in *Memories and Milestones* in 1915.

"Emerson" was published in *Atlantic Monthly*, January–February 1897, and reprinted in *Emerson and Other Essays* in 1898.

"Robert Browning" was published in *Emerson and Other Essays* in 1898.

Acknowledgments

Many persons have been kind to me during the preparation of this volume. I wish particularly to thank Jacques Barzun for his illuminating foreword and for advice and help going back more than a decade. I am also grateful to Charles Moritz and Edward Chalfant for the close reading they gave my introduction. Their strictures and suggestions proved indispensable. In the course of my work I was privileged to establish an epistolary friendship with the late Melvin H. Bernstein, the distinguished Chapman scholar. Richard Hovey, who has also written memorably on Chapman, has been similarly helpful. My friend and colleague Susan Wool did expert translations of quotations Chapman left in the original in his essay on Balzac. Evelyn Delannoy, another good friend and co-worker, skillfully input the manuscript on computer disk.

I am deeply grateful to Helen Chalfant and Emile and Keitha Capouya for their faith in me and Chapman. I have also received encouragement from John Winthrop Aldrich, cousin to the Chapman family. John Harding showed me Chapman materials in the archives of the Century Association.

My dear friend William Humphrey passed away soon after this book found the right publisher. Bill's writings and his friendship are things I shall always cherish. His widow, Dorothy, encouraged me in the very same way.

The late Chanler Chapman befriended me when I expressed interest in his father's work. This volume is offered in fond remembrance of Chanler's hospitality and irrepressible spirit. I wish also to thank my dear parents for numberless kindnesses to me during my time with John Jay Chapman and before.

Richard Wentworth and the staff of the University of Illinois Press have been unstinting in their support and help. I thank them wholeheartedly.

The essays in this anthology follow the versions printed in *The Collected Works of John Jay Chapman,* published by M and S Press in 1970. The unpublished letters of John Jay Chapman were transcribed by M. A. DeWolfe Howe and are published here by permission of the Houghton Library. I wish to thank Rodney Dennis, curator of manuscripts at the library, for this permission.

Unbought Spirit

Coatesville

We are met to commemorate the anniversary of one of the most dreadful crimes in history—not for the purpose of condemning it, but to repent of our share in it. We do not start any agitation with regard to that particular crime. I understand that an attempt to prosecute the chief criminals has been made, and has entirely failed; because the whole community, and in a sense our whole people, are really involved in the guilt. The failure of the prosecution in this case, in all such cases, is only a proof of the magnitude of the guilt, and of the awful fact that everyone shares in it.

I will tell you why I am here; I will tell you what happened to me. When I read in the newspapers of August 14, a year ago, about the burning alive of a human being, and of how a few desperate, fiend-minded men had been permitted to torture a man chained to an iron bedstead, burning alive, thrust back by pitchforks when he struggled out of it, while around about stood hundreds of well-dressed American citizens, both from the vicinity and from afar, coming on foot and in wagons, assembling on telephone call, as if by magic, silent, whether from terror or indifference, fascinated and impotent, hundreds of persons watch-

I

ing this awful sight and making no attempt to stay the wickedness, and no one man among them all who was inspired to risk his life in an attempt to stop it, no one man to name the name of Christ, of humanity, of government! As I read the newspaper accounts of the scene enacted here in Coatesville a year ago, I seemed to get a glimpse into the unconscious soul of this country. I saw a seldom revealed picture of the American heart and of the American nature. I seemed to be looking into the heart of the criminal—a cold thing, an awful thing.

I said to myself, "I shall forget this, we shall all forget it; but it will be there. What I have seen is not an illusion. It is the truth. I have seen death in the heart of this people." For to look at the agony of a fellow-being and remain aloof means death in the heart of the onlooker. Religious fanaticism has sometimes lifted men to the frenzy of such cruelty, political passion has sometimes done it, personal hatred might do it, the excitement of the amphitheater in the degenerate days of Roman luxury could do it. But here an audience chosen by chance in America has stood spellbound through an improvised *auto-da-fé*, irregular, illegal, having no religious significance, not sanctioned by custom, having no immediate provocation, the audience standing by merely in cold dislike.

I saw during one moment something beyond all argument in the depth of its significance. You might call it the paralysis of the nerves about the heart in a people habitually and unconsciously given over to selfish aims, an ignorant people who knew not what spectacle they were providing, or what part they were playing in a judgment-play which history was exhibiting on that day.

No theories about the race problem, no statistics, legislation, or mere educational endeavor, can quite meet the lack which that day revealed in the American people. For what we saw was death. The people stood like blighted things, like ghosts about Acheron, waiting for someone or something to determine their destiny for them.

Whatever life itself is, that thing must be replenished in us. The opposite of hate is love, the opposite of cold is heat; what we need is the love of God and reverence for human nature. For one moment I knew that I had seen our true need; and I was afraid that I should forget it and that I should go about framing arguments and agitations and starting schemes of education, when the need was deeper than education. And I became filled with one idea, that I must not forget what I had seen, and that I must do something to remember it. And I am here to-day chiefly that I may remember that vision. It seems fitting to come to this town where the crime occurred and hold a prayer-meeting, so that our hearts may be turned to God through whom mercy may flow into us.

Let me say one thing more about the whole matter. The subject we are dealing with is not local. The act, to be sure, took place at Coatesville and everyone looked to Coatesville to follow it up. Some months ago I asked a friend who lives not far from here something about this case, and about the expected prosecutions, and he replied to me: "It wasn't in my county," and that made me wonder whose county it was in. And it seemed to be in my county. I live on the Hudson River; but I knew that this great wickedness that happened in Coatesville is not the wickedness of Coatesville nor of to-day. It is the wickedness of all America and of three hundred years—the wickedness of the slave trade. All of us are tinctured by it. No special place, no special persons, are to blame. A nation cannot practice a course of inhuman crime for three hundred years and then suddenly throw off the effects of it. Less than fifty years ago domestic slavery was abolished among us; and in one way and another the marks of that vice are in our faces. There is no country in Europe where the Coatesville tragedy or anything remotely like it could have been enacted, probably no country in the world.

On the day of the calamity, those people in the automobiles came by the hundred and watched the torture, and passers-by came in a great multitude and watched it—and did nothing. On the next morning the newspapers spread the news and spread the paralysis until the whole country seemed to be helplessly watching this awful murder, as awful as anything ever done on the earth; and the whole of our people seemed to be looking on helplessly, not able to respond, not knowing what to do next. That spectacle has been in my mind.

The trouble has come down to us out of the past. The only reason that slavery is wrong is that it is cruel and makes men cruel and leaves them cruel. Someone may say that you and I cannot repent because we did not do the act. But we are involved in it. We are still looking on. Do you not see that this whole event is merely the last parable, the most vivid, the most terrible illustration that ever was given by man or imagined by a Jewish prophet, of the relation between good and evil in this world, and of the relation of men to one another?

This whole matter has been an historic episode; but it is a part, not only of our national history, but of the personal history of each one of us. With the great disease (slavery) came the climax (the war), and after the climax gradually began the cure, and in the process of cure comes now the knowledge of what the evil was. I say that our need is new life, and that books and resolutions will not save us, but only such disposition in our hearts and souls as will enable the new life, love, force, hope, virtue, which surround us always, to enter into us.

This is the discovery that each man must make for himself—the discovery that what he really stands in need of he cannot get for himself, but must wait till God gives it to him. I have felt the impulse to come here to-day to testify to this truth.

The occasion is not small; the occasion looks back on three centuries and embraces a hemisphere. Yet the occasion is small compared with the truth it leads us to. For this truth touches all ages and affects every soul in the world.

[1912]

Politics

Misgovernment in the United States is an incident in the history of commerce. It is part of the triumph of industrial progress. Its details are easier to understand if studied as a part of the commercial development of the country than if studied as a part of government, because many of the wheels and cranks in the complex machinery of government are now performing functions so perverted as to be unmeaning from the point of view of political theory, but which become perfectly plain if looked at from the point of view of trade.

The growth and concentration of capital which the railroad and the telegraph made possible is the salient fact in the history of the last quarter-century. That fact is at the bottom of our political troubles. It was inevitable that the enormous masses of wealth, springing out of new conditions and requiring new laws, should strive to control the legislation and the administration which touched them at every point. At the present time, we cannot say just what changes were or were not required by enlightened theory. It is enough to see that such changes as came were inevitable; and nothing can blind us to the fact that the methods by which they were obtained were subversive of free government.

Whatever form of government had been in force in America during this era would have run the risk of being controlled by capital, of being bought and run for revenue. It happened that the beginning of the period found the machinery of our government in a particularly purchasable state. The war had left the people divided into two parties which were fanatically hostile to each other. The people were party mad. Party name and party symbols were of an almost religious importance.

At the very moment when the enthusiasm of the nation had been exhausted in a heroic war which left the Republican party-managers in possession of the ark of the covenant, the best intellect of the country was withdrawn from public affairs and devoted to trade. During the period of expansion which followed, the industrial forces called in the ablest men of the nation to aid them in getting control of the machinery of government. The name of king was never freighted with more power than the name of party in the United States; whatever was done in that name was right. It is the old story: there has never been a despotism which did not rest upon superstition. The same spirit that made the Republican name all powerful in the nation at large made the Democratic name valuable in Democratic districts.

The situation as it existed was made to the hand of trade. Political power had by the war been condensed and packed for delivery; and in the natural course of things the political trademarks began to find their way into the coffers of the capitalist. The change of motive power behind the party organizations—from principles, to money—was silently effected during the thirty years which followed the war. Like all organic change, it was unconscious. It was understood by no one. It is recorded only in a few names and phrases; as, for instance, that part of the organization which was purchased was called the "machine," and the general manager of it became known as the "boss." The external political history of the country continued as before. It is true that a steady degradation was to be seen in public life, a steady failure of character, a steady decline of decency. But questions continued to be discussed, and in form decided, on their merits, because it was in the interest of commerce that they should in form be so decided. Only quite recently has the control of money become complete; and there are reasons for believing that the climax is past.

Let us take a look at the change on a small scale. A railroad is to be run through a country town or small city, in New York or Pennsylvania. The railroad employs a local attorney, naturally the ablest attorney in the place. As time goes on, various permits for street uses are needed; and instead of relying solely upon popular demand, the attorney finds it easier to bribe the proper officials. All goes well: the railroad thrives, the town grows. But in the course of a year new permits of various kinds are needed. The town ordinances interfere with the road and require amendment. There is to be a town election; and it occurs to the railroad's attorney that he might be in alliance with the town officers before they are elected. He goes to the managers of the party which is likely to win; for instance, the Republican party. Everything that the railroad wants is really called for by the economic needs of the town. The railroad wants only fair play and no factious obstruction. The attorney talks to the Republican leader, and has a chance to look over the list of candidates, and perhaps even to select some of them. The railroad makes the largest campaign subscription ever made in that part of the country. The Republican leader can now employ more workers to man the polls, and, if necessary, he can buy votes. He must also retain some fraction of the contribution for his own support, and distribute the rest in such manner as will best keep his "organization" together.

The party wins, and the rights of the railroad are secured for a year. It is true that the brother of the Republican leader is employed on the road as a brakeman; but he is a competent man.

During the year, a very nice point of law arises as to the rights of the railroad to certain valuable land claimed by the town. The city attorney is an able man, and reasonable. In spite of his ability, he manages somehow to state the city's case on an untenable ground. A decision follows in favor of the railroad. At the following election, the city attorney has become the Republican candidate for judge, and the railroad's campaign subscription is trebled. In the conduct of railroads, even under the best management, accidents are common; and while it is true that important decisions are appealable, a trial judge has enormous powers which are practically discretionary. Meanwhile, there have arisen questions of local taxation of the railroad's property, questions as to grade crossings, as to the lighting of cars, as to time schedules, and the like. The court calendars are becoming crowded with railroad business; and that business is now more than one attorney can attend to. In fact, the half dozen local lawyers of prominence are railroad men; the rest of the lawyers would like to be. Every one of the railroad lawyers receives deferential treatment, and, when possible, legal advantage in all of the public offices. The community is now in the control of a ring, held together by just one thing, the railroad company's subscription to the campaign fund.

By this time a serious scandal has occurred in the town,—nothing less than the rumor of a deficit in the town treasurer's accounts, and the citizens are concerned about it. One of the railroad's lawyers, a strong party man, happens to be occupying the post of district attorney; for the yearly campaign subscriptions continue. This district attorney is, in fact, one of the committee on nominations who put the town treasurer into office; and the Republican party is responsible for both. No prosecution follows. The district attorney stands for re-election.

An outsider comes to live in the town. He wants to reform things, and proceeds to talk politics. He is not so inexperienced as to seek aid from the rich and respectable classes. He knows that the men who subscribed to the railroad's stock are the same men who own the local bank, and that the manufacturers and other business men of the place rely on the bank for carrying on their business. He knows that all trades which are specially touched by the law, such as the liquor-dealers' and hotel-keepers', must "stand in" with the administration; so also must the small shopkeepers, and those who have to do with sidewalk privileges and town ordinances generally. The newcomer talks to the leading hardware merchant, a man of stainless reputation, who admits that the district attorney has been remiss; but the merchant is a Republican, and says that so long as he lives he will vote for the party that saved the country. To vote for a Democrat is a crime. The reformer next approaches the druggist (whose father-in-law is in the employ of the railroad), and receives the same reply. He goes to the florist. But the florist owns a piece of real estate, and has a theory that it is assessed too high. The time for revising the assessment rolls is coming near, and he has to see the authorities about that. The florist agrees that the town is a den of thieves; but he must live; he has no time to go into theoretical politics. The stranger next interviews a retired grocer. But the grocer has lent money to his nephew, who is in the coal business, and is getting special rates from the railroad, and is paying off the debt rapidly. The grocer would be willing to help, but his name must not be used.

It is needless to multiply instances of what every one knows. After canvassing the whole community, the stranger finds five persons who are willing to work to defeat the district attorney: a young doctor of good education and small practice, a young lawyer who thinks he can make use of the movement by betraying it, a retired anti-slavery preacher, a maiden lady, and a piano-tuner. The district attorney is re-elected by an overwhelming vote.

All this time the railroad desires only a quiet life. It takes no interest in politics. It is making money, and does not want values disturbed. It is conservative.

In the following year worse things happen. The town treasurer steals more money, and the district attorney is openly accused of sharing the profits. The Democrats are shouting for reform, and declare that they will run the strongest man in town for district attorney. He is a Democrat, but one who fought for the Union. He is no longer in active practice, and is, on the whole, the most distinguished citizen of the place. This suggestion is popular. The hardware merchant declares that he will vote the Democratic ticket, and there is a sensation. It appears that during all these years there has been a Democratic organization in the town, and that the notorious corruption of the Republicans makes a Democratic victory possible. The railroad company therefore goes to the manager of the Democratic party, and explains that it wants only to be let alone. It explains that it takes no interest in politics, but that, if a change is to come, it desires only that So-and-So shall be retained, and it leaves a subscription with the Democratic manager. In short, it makes the best terms it can. The Democratic leader, if he thinks that he can make a clean sweep, may nominate the distinguished citizen, together with a group of his own organization comrades. It obviously would be of no use to him to name a full citizens' ticket. That would be treason to his party. If he takes this course and wins, we shall have ring rule of a slightly milder type. The course begins anew, under a Democratic name; and it may be several years before another malfeasance occurs.

But the Republican leader and the railroad company do not want war; they want peace. They may agree to make it worth while for the Democrats not to run the distinguished citizen. A few Democrats are let into the Republican ring. They are promised certain minor appointive offices, and some contracts and emoluments. Accordingly, the Democrats do not nominate the distinguished citizen. The hardware man sees little choice between the two nominees for district attorney; at any rate, he will not vote for a machine Democrat, and he again votes for his party nominee. All the reform talk simmers down to silence. The Republicans are returned to power.

The town is now ruled by a Happy Family. Stable equilibrium has been reached at last. Commercialism is in control. Henceforth, the railroad company pays the bills for keeping up both party organizations, and it receives care and protection from whichever side is nominally in power.

The party leaders have by this time become the general utility men of the railroad; they are its agents and factotums. The boss is the handy man of the capitalist. So long as the people of the town are content to vote on party lines they cannot get away from the railroad. In fact, there are no national parties in the town. A man may talk about them, but he cannot vote for one of them, because they do not exist. He can vote only for or against the railroad; and to do the latter, an independent ticket must be nominated.

It must not be imagined that any part of the general public clearly understands this situation. The state of mind of the Better Element of the Republican side has been seen. The good Democrats are equally distressed. The distinguished citizen ardently desires to oust the Republican ring. He subscribes year after year to the campaign fund of his own party, and declares that the defalcation of the town treasurer has given it the opportunity of a generation. The Democratic organization takes his money and accepts his moral support, and uses it to build up one end of the machine. It cries, "Reform! Reform! Give us back the principles of Jefferson and of Tilden!"

The Boss-out-of-Power must welcome all popular movements. He must sometimes accept a candidate from a citizens' committee, sometimes refuse to do so. He must spread his mainsail to the national party wind of the moment. His immense advantage is an intellectual one. He alone knows the principles of the game. He alone sees that the power of the bosses comes from party loyalty. Croker recently stated his case frankly thus: "A man who would desert his party would desert his country."

It may be remarked, in passing, that New York city reached the Happy Family stage many years ago. Tammany Hall is in power, being maintained there by the great mercantile interests. The Republican party is out of power, and its organization is kept going by the same interests. It has always been the ear-mark of an enterprise of the first financial magnitude in New York that it subscribed to both campaign funds. The Republican function has been to prevent any one from disturbing Tammany Hall. This has not been difficult; the Republicans have always been in a hopeless minority, and the machine managers have understood this perfectly. Now if, by the simple plan of denouncing Tammany Hall, and appealing to the war record of the Republican party, they could minimize the independent vote and hold their own constituency, Tammany would be safe. The matter is actually more complex than this, but the principle is obvious.

To return to our country town. It is easy to see that the railroad is pouring out its money in the systematic corruption of the entire community. Even the offices with which it has no contact will be affected by this corruption. Men put in office because they are tools will work as tools only. Voters once bribed will thereafter vote for money only. The subscribing and the voting classes, whose state of mind is outlined above, are not purely mercenary. The retired grocer, the florist, the druggist, are all influenced by mixed motives, in which personal interest bears a greater or a smaller share. Each of these men belongs to a party, as a Brahmin is born into a caste. His spirit must suffer an agony of conversion before he can get free, even if he is poor. If he has property, he must pay for that conversion by the loss of money, also.

Since 1865 the towns throughout the United States have been passing through this stage. A ring was likely to spring up wherever there was available capital. We hear a great talk about the failure of our institutions as applied to cities, as if it were our incapacity to deal with masses of people and with the problems of city expansion that wrecked us. It is nothing of the sort. There is intellect and business capacity enough in the country to run the Chinese Empire like clockwork. Philosophers state broadly that our people "prefer to live in towns," and cite the rush to the cities during the last thirty years. The truth is that the exploitation of the continent could be done most conveniently by the assembling of business men in towns; and hence it is that the worst rings are found in the larger cities. But there are rings everywhere; and wherever you see one you will find a factory behind it. If the population had remained scattered, commerce would have pursued substantially the same course. We should have had the rings just the same. It is perfectly true that the wonderful and scientific concentration of business that we have seen in the past thirty years gave the chance for the wonderful and scientific concentration of its control over politics. The state machine could be constructed easily, by consolidating local rings of the same party name.

[1898]

Between Elections

An election is like a flash of lightning at midnight. You get an instantaneous photograph of what every man is doing. You see his real relation toward his government. But an election happens only once a year. Government goes on day and night.

It is hard breaking down the popular fallacy that there is such a thing as "politics," governed by peculiar conditions, which must be understood and respected; that the whole thing is a mystic avocation, run as a trade by high priests and low priests, and is remote from our daily life. Our system of party government has been developed with the aim of keeping the control in the hands of professionals. Technicalities have been multiplied, and the rules of the game have become more and more complex. There exists, consequently, an unformulated belief that the corruption of politics is something by itself. Yet there probably never was a civilization where the mesh of all powers and interests was so close. It is like the interlocking of roots in a swamp. Such density and cohesion were never seen in any epoch, such a mat and tangle of personalities, where every man is tied up with the fibres of every other. If you take an axe or a saw, and cut a clean piece out of it anywhere, you will maim every member of society. How idle, then, even to think of politics as a subject by itself, or of the corruptions of the times as localized! Politics gives what the chemists call a "mirror," and shows the ingredients in the average man's composition. But you must take your mind off politics if you want to understand America. You must take up the lives of individuals and follow them out, as they play against each other in counterpoint. As soon as you do this you will not be able to determine where politics begins and where it stops. It is all politics: it is all social intercourse: it is all business. Any square foot of this soil will give you the whole fauna and flora of the land. Where will you put in your wedge of reform? There is not a cranny anywhere. The mass is like crude copper ore that cannot be blasted. It blows out the charge.

We think that political agitation must show political results. This is like trying to alter the shape of a shadow without touching its object. The hope is not only mistaken, it is absurd. The results to be obtained from reform movements cannot show in the political field till they have passed through the social world.

"But, after all, what you want is votes, is it not?" "It would be so encouraging to see virtue win, that everybody would vote for you thereafter. Why don't you manage it somehow?" This sort of talk is the best record of incompetence which corruption has imprinted. Enlighten this class and you have saved the Republic. Why, my friend, you are so lost, you are so much a mere product of tyranny that you do not know what a vote is. True, we want votes, but the votes we want must be cast spontaneously. We do not want them so badly as to buy them. A vote is only important because it is an opinion. Even a dictator cannot force opinions upon his subjects by six months of rule; and yet the complaint is that decency gets few votes after a year of effort by a handful of radicals who are despised by the community. We only enter the field of politics because we can there get a hearing. The candidates in reform movements are tools. They are like crowbars that break open the mind of the age. They cannot be dodged, concealed, or laughed away. Every one is aroused from his lethargy by seeing a real man walk on the scene, amid all the stage properties and marionettes of conventional politics. "Not fair!" the people cry. They do not vote for him, of course, but they talk about the portent with a vigor no mere doctrine could call forth, and the discussion blossoms at a later date into a new public spirit, a new and genuine demand for better things.

It is apparent that between the initial political activity of reformers and their ultimate political accomplishments, there must intervene the real agitation, the part that does the work, which goes on in the brains and souls of individual men, and which can only be observed in social life, in manners and conversation.

Now let us take up the steps by which, in practical life, the reaction is set going. Enter the nearest coterie of radicals and listen to the quarrel. Reformers proverbially disagree, and "their sects mince themselves almost to atoms." With us the quarrel always arises over the same point. "Can we afford, under these particular circumstances, to tell the exact truth?" I have never known a reform movement in which this discussion did not rage from start to finish, nor have I known one where any other point was involved. You are a citizens' committee. The parties offer to give you half a loaf. Well and good. But this is not their main object. They want you to call it a whole loaf. They want to dissipate your agitation by getting you to tell the public that you are satisfied. What they hate is the standard. The war between you and them is a spiritual game of chess. They must get you to say they are right. It is their only means of retaining their power.

Thus the apple of discord falls into the Reform camp. Half its members take the bait. In New York City our politics have been so picturesque, the pleas of the politician so shallow, the lies demanded from the reformers so obvious, that the eternal principles of the situation have been revealed in their elemental simplicity. It is just because the impulse towards better things carries no material content—we do not want any particular thing, but we want an improvement in everything—it is just because the whole movement is purely moral, that the same questions always arise.

We ought not to grieve over the discussion, over the heart-burn and heated argument that start from a knot of radicals and run through the community, setting men against each other. The quarrel in the executive committee of this reform body is the initiative of much wholesome life. They are no more responsible for it, they can no more avoid it, the community can no more advance to higher standards before they have had it, than a child can skate before it can walk.

The executive committee is discussing the schools. In consequence of a recent agitation, the politicians have put up a candidate who will give new plumbing, even if he does steal the books, and the question is whether the School Association shall indorse this candidate. If it does, he wins. If it does not, both plumbing and books are likely to remain the prey of the other party, and the Lord knows how bad that is. The fight rages in the committee, and some sincere old gentleman is prophesying typhoid.

The practical question is: "Do you want good plumbing, or do you want the truth?" You cannot have both this year. If the association goes out and tells the public exactly what it knows, it will get itself laughed at, insult the candidate, and elect his opponent. If it tells the truth, it might as well run a candidate of its own as a protest and an advertisement of that truth. It can buy good plumbing with a lie, and the old gentleman thinks it ought to do so. The reformers are going to endorse the candidate, and upon their heads will be visited his theft of the books. They have sold out the little public confidence they held. Had they stood out for another year, under the practical régime which they had already endured for twenty, and had they devoted themselves to augmenting the public interest in the school question, both parties would have offered them plumbing and books to allay the excitement. The parties might, perhaps, have relaxed their grip on the whole school system rather than meet the issue.

But the Association does not understand this. It does not, as yet, clearly know its own mind. All this procedure, this going forward and back, is necessary. The community must pass through these experiences before it discovers that the shortest road to good schools is truth. A few men learn by each turn of the wheel, and these men tend to consolidate. They become a sort of school of political thought. They see that they do not care a whit more about the schools than they do about the parks; that the school agitation is a handy way to make the citizens take notice of maladministration in all departments; that the parties may be left to reform themselves, and to choose the most telling bid for popular favor; that the parties must do this and will do this, in so far as the public demands it, and will not do it under any other circumstances.

It is the very greatest folly in the world for an agitator to be content with a partial success. It destroys his cause. He fades instantly. You cannot see him. He is become part of the corrupt and contented public. His business is to make others demand good administration. He must never reap, but always sow. Let him leave the reaping to others. There will be many of them, and their material accomplishments will be the same whether he endorses them or not. If by chance some party, some administration gives him one hundred per cent of what he demands, let him acknowledge it handsomely; but he need not thank them. They did it because they had to, or because their conscience compelled them. In neither case was it done for him.

In other words, reform is an idea that must be taken up as a whole. You do not want any specific thing. You use every issue as a symbol. Let us give up the hope of finding any simpler way out of it. Let us take up the burden at its heaviest end, and acknowledge that nothing but an increase of personal force in every American can change our politics. It is curious that this course, which is the shortest cut to the millennium, should be met with the reproach that it puts off victory. This is entirely due to a defect in the imagination of people who are dealing with an unfamiliar subject. We have to learn its principles. We know that what we really want is all of virtue; but it seems so unreasonable to claim this, that we try to buy it piecemeal,—item, a schoolhouse, item, four parks; and with each gain comes a sacrifice of principle, disintegration, discouragement. Fools, if you had asked for all, you would have had this and more. We are defeated by compromise because, no matter how much we may deceive ourselves into thinking that good government is an aggregate of laws and parks, it is not true. Good government is the outcome of private virtue, and virtue is one thing,—a unit, a force, a mode of motion. It cannot pass through a non-conductor of casuistry at any point. Compromise is loss: first, because it stops the movement, and kills energy; second, because it encourages the illusion that the wooden schoolhouse is good government. As against this, you have the fact that some hundreds of school children do get housed six months before they would have been housed otherwise. But this is like cashing a draft for a thousand pounds with a dish of oatmeal.

We have, perhaps, followed in the wake of some little Reform movement, and it has left us with an insight into the relation between private opinion and public occurrences. We have really found out two things: first, that in order to have better government, the talk and private intelligence upon which it rests must be going forward all the time; and second, that the individual conscience, intelligence, or private will is always set free by the same process,—to wit, by the telling of truth. The identity between public and private life reveals itself the instant a man adopts the plan of indiscriminate truthtelling. He unmasks batteries and discloses wires at every dinner-party; he sees practical politics in every law office, and social influence in every convention; and wherever he is, he suddenly finds himself, by his own will or against it, a centre of forces. Let him blurt out his opinion. Instantly there follows a little flash of reality. The shams drop, and the lines of human influence, the vital currents of energy, are disclosed. The only difference between a reform movement, so-called, and the private act of any man who desires to better conditions, is that the private man sets one drawing-room in a ferment by speaking his mind or by cutting his friend, and the agitator sets ten thousand in a ferment by attacking the age.

As a practical matter, the conduct of politics depends upon the dinner-table talk of men who are not in politics at all. Government is carried on from moment to moment by the people. The executive is a mere hand and arm. For instance, there is a public excitement about Civil Service Reform. A law is passed and is being evaded. If the governor is to set it up again, he must be sustained by the public. They must follow and understand the situation or the official is helpless. But do we sustain him? We do not. We are half-hearted. To lend power to his hand we shall have to be strong men. If we now stood ready to denounce him for himself falling short by the breadth of a hair of his whole duty, our support, when we gave it, would be worth having. But we are starchless, and deserve a starchless service.

What did you find out at the last meeting of the Library Committee? You found out that Commissioner Hopkins's nephew was in the piano business; hence the commissioner's views on the music question. Repeat it to the first man you meet in the street, and bring it up at the next meeting of the committee. You did not think you had much influence in town politics, and hardly knew how to step in. Yet the town seems to have no time for any other subject than your attack on the commissioner. From this point on you begin to understand conditions. Every man in town reveals his real character, and his real relation to the town wickedness and to the universe by the way he treats you. You are beginning to get near to something real and something interesting. There is no one in the United States, no matter how small a town he lives in, or how inconspicuous he or she is, who does not have three invitations a week to enter practical politics by such a door as this. It makes no difference whether he regard himself as a scientific man studying phenomena, or a saint purifying society; he will become both. There is no way to study sociology but this. The books give no hint of what the science is like. They are written by men who do not know the world, but who go about gleaning information instead of trying experiments.

The first discovery we make is that the worst enemy of good government is not our ignorant foreign voter, but our educated domestic railroad president, our prominent business man, our leading lawyer. If there is any truth in the optimistic belief that our standards are now going up, we shall soon see proofs of it in our homes. We shall not note our increase of virtue so much by seeing more crooks in Sing Sing, as by seeing fewer of them in the drawing-rooms. You can acquire more knowledge of American politics by attacking, in open talk, a political lawyer of social standing, than you can in a year of study. These backstair men are in every Bar Association and every Reform Club. They are the agents who supervise the details of corruption. They run between the capitalist, the boss, and the public official. They know as fact what every one else knows as inference. They are the priestly class of commerce, and correspond to the intriguing ecclesiastics in periods of church ascendency. Some want money, some office, some mere power, others want social prominence; and their art is to play off interest against interest and advance themselves.

As the president of a social club I have a power that I can use against my party boss or for him. If he can count upon me to serve him at need, it is a gain to him to have me establish myself as a reformer. The most dependable of these confidence men (for they betray nobody, and are universally used and trusted) can amass money and stand in the forefront of social life; and now and then one of them is made an archbishop or a foreign minister. They are, indeed, the figure-heads of the age, the essence of all the wickedness and degradation of our times. So long as such men enjoy public confidence we shall remain as we are. They must be deposed in the public mind.

And yet these gentlemen are the weakest point in the serried ranks of iniquity. They are weak because they have social ambition, and the place to reach them is in their clubs. They are the best possible object lessons, because everybody knows them. Social punishment is the one cruel reality, the one terrible weapon, the one judgment against which lawyers cannot protect a man. It is as silent as theft, and it raises the cry of "Stop thief!" like a burglar alarm.

The general cowardice of this age covers itself with the illusion of charity, and asks, in the name of Christ, that no one's feelings be hurt. But there is not in the New Testament any hint that hypocrites are to be treated with charity. This class is so intrenched on all sides that the enthusiasts cannot touch them. Their elbows are interlocked; they sit cheek by jowl with virtue. They are rich; they possess the earth. How shall we strike them? Very easily. They are so soft with feeding on politic lies that they drop dead if you give them a dose of ridicule in a drawing-room. Denunciation is well enough, but laughter is the true ratsbane for hypocrites. If you set off a few jests, the air is changed. The men themselves cannot laugh or be laughed at; for nature's revenge has given them masks for faces. You may see a whole room full of them crack with pain because they cannot laugh. They are angry, and do not speak.

Everybody in America is soft, and hates conflict. The cure for this, both in politics and social life, is the same,—hardihood. Give them raw truth. They think they will die. Their friends call you a murderer. Four thousand ladies and eighty bank directors brought vinegar and brown paper to Low when he was attacked, and Roosevelt posed as a martyr because it was said, up and down, that he acted the part of a selfish politician. What humbug! How is it that all these things grow on the same root,—fraud, cowardice, formality, sentimentalism, and a lack of humor? Why do people become so solemn when they are making a deal, and so angry when they are defending it? The righteous indignation expended in protecting Roosevelt would have founded a church.

The whole problem of better government is a question of how to get people to stop simpering and saying "After you" to cant. A is an aristocrat. B is a boss. C is a candidate. D is a distiller. E is an excellent citizen. They dine. Gloomy silence would be more respectable than this chipper concern that all shall go well.

Is not this politics? Yes, and the very essence of it. Is not the exposure of it practical reform? How easily the arrow goes in! A does not think you should confound him with B, nor E with C. Each is a reformer when he looks to the right, and a scamp as seen from the left. What is their fault? Collusion. "But A means so well." They all mean well. Let us not confound the gradations of their virtue; but can we call any one an honest man who knowingly consorts with thieves? This they all do. Let us declare it. Their resentment at finding themselves classed together drives the wedge into the clique.

Remember, too, that there is no such thing as abstract truth. You must talk facts, you must name names, you must impute motives. You must say what is in your mind. It is the only means you have of cutting yourself free from the body of this death. Innuendo will not do. Nobody minds innuendo. We live and breathe nothing else. If you are not strong enough to face the issue in private life, do not dream that you can do anything for public affairs. This, of course, means fight, not to-morrow, but now. It is only in the course of conflict that any one can come to understand the system, the habit of thought, the mental condition, out of which all our evils arise. The first difficulty is to see the evils clearly; and when we do see them it is like fighting an atmosphere to contend against them. They are so universal and omnipresent that you have no terms to name them by. You must burn a disinfectant.

We have observed, thus far, that no question is ever involved in practical agitation except truth-telling. So long as a man is trying to tell the truth, his remarks will contain a margin which other people will regard as mystifying and irritating exaggeration. It is this very margin of controversy that does the work. The more accurate he is, the less he exaggerates, the more he will excite people. It is only by the true part of what is said that the interest is roused. No explosion follows a lie.

The awaking of the better feelings of the individual man is not only the immediate but the ultimate end of all politics. Nor need we be alarmed at any collateral results. No one has ever succeeded in drawing any valid distinction between positive and negative educational work, except this: that in so far as a man is positive himself, he does positive work. It is necessary to destroy reputations when they are lies. Peace be to their ashes. But war and fire until they be ashes. This is positive and constructive work. You cannot state your case without using popular illustrations, and in clearing the ground for justice and mercy, some little great man gets shown up as a make-believe. This is constructive work.

It is impossible to do harm to reform, unless you are taking some course that tends to put people to sleep. Strangely enough, the great outcry is made upon occasions when men are refusing to take such a course. This is due to the hypnotism of self-interest. "Don't wake us up!" they cry, "We cannot stand the agony of it;" and the rising energy with which they speak wakes other sleepers. In the early stages of any new idea the only advertising it gets is denunciation. This is so much better than silence, that one may hail it as the dawn. You must speak till you draw blood. The agitators have always understood this. Such men as Wendell Phillips were not extravagant. They were practical men. Their business was to get heard. They used vitriol, but they were dealing with the hide of the rhinoceros.

[1900]

The Unity of Human Nature*

If one could stand on the edge of the moon and look down through a couple of thousand years on human politics, it would be apparent that everything that happened on the earth was directly dependent on everything else that happened there. Whether the Italian peasant shall eat salt with his bread, depends upon Bismarck. Whether the prison system of Russia shall be improved, depends upon the ministry of Great Britain. If Lord Beaconsfield is in power, there is no leisure in Russia for domestic reform. The lash is everywhere lifted in a security furnished by the concurrence of all the influences upon the globe that favor coercion. In like manner, the good things that happen are each the product of all extant conditions. Constitutional government in England qualifies the whole of western Europe. Our slaves were not set free without the assistance of every liberal mind in Europe; and the thoughts which we think in our closet affect the fate of the Boer in South Africa. That Tolstoy is to-day living unmolested upon his farm instead of serving in a Siberian mine, that Dreyfus is alive and not dead, is due directly to

*This was an address delivered before the graduating class at Hobart College in 1900. [Chapman included this note when the essay was printed in 1910.]

the people in this audience and to others like them scattered over Europe and America.

The effect of enlightenment on tyranny is not merely to make the tyrant afraid to be cruel, it makes him not want to be cruel. It makes him see what cruelty is. And reciprocally the effect of cruelty on enlightenment is to make that enlightenment grow dim. It prevents men from seeing what cruelty is.

The Czar of Russia cannot get rid of your influence, nor you of his. Every ukase he signs makes allowance for you, and, on the other hand, the whole philosophy of your life is tinged by him. You believe that the abuses under the Russian government are inscrutably different from and worse than our own; whereas both sets of atrocities are identical in principle, and are more alike in fact, in taste and smell and substance than your prejudice is willing to admit. The existence of Russia narrows America's philosophy, and misconduct by a European power may be seen reflected in the moral tone of your clergyman on the following day. More Americans have abandoned their faith in free government since England began to play the tyrant in South Africa than there were colonists in the country in 1776.

Europe is all one family, and speaks, one might say, the same language. The life that has been transplanted to North America during the last three centuries, is European life. From your position on the moon you would not be able to understand what the supposed differences were between European and American things, that the Americans make so much fuss over. You would say, "I see only one people, splashed over different continents. The problems they talk about, the houses they live in, the clothes they wear, seem much alike. Their education and catchwords are identical. They are the children of the Classics, of Christianity, and of the Revival of Learning. They are homogeneous, and they are growing more homogeneous."

The subtle influences that modern nations exert over one another illustrate the unity of life on the globe. But if we turn to ancient history we find in its bare outlines staggering proof of the interdependence of nations. The Greeks were wiped out.

The Unity of Human Nature

They could not escape their contemporaries any more than we can escape the existence of the Malays. Israel could not escape Assyria, nor Assyria Persia, nor Persia Macedonia, nor Macedonia Rome, nor Rome the Goths. Life is not a boarding-school where a bad boy can be dismissed for the benefit of the rest. He remains. He must be dealt with. He is as much here as we are ourselves. The whole of Europe and Asia and South America and every Malay and every Chinaman, Hindoo, Tartar, and Tagal—of such is our civilization.

Let us for the moment put aside every dictate of religion and political philosophy. Let us discard all prejudice and all love. Let us regard nothing except facts. Does not the coldest conclusion of science announce the fact that the world is peopled, and that every individual of that population has an influence as certain and far more discoverable than the influence of the weight of his body upon the solar system?

A Chinaman lands in San Francisco. The Constitution of the United States begins to rock and tremble. What shall we do with him? The deepest minds of the past must be ransacked to the bottom to find an answer. Every one of seventy million Americans must pass through a throe of thought that leaves him a modified man. The same thing is true when the American lands in China. These creatures have thus begun to think of each other. It is unimaginable that they should not hereafter incessantly and never-endingly continue to think of each other. And out of their thoughts grows the destiny of mankind.

We have an inherited and stupid notion that the East does not change. If Japan goes through a transformation scene under our eyes, we still hold to our prejudice as to the immutability of the Chinese. If our own people and the European nations seem to be meeting and surging and reappearing in unaccustomed rôles every ten years, till modern history looks like a fancy ball, we still go on muttering some old ignorant shibboleth about East and West, Magna Charta, the Indian Mutiny, and Mahomet. The chances are that England will be dead-letter, and Russia progressive before we have done talking. Of a truth, when we consider the rapidity of visible change and the amplitude of time—for there is plenty of time—we need not despair of progress.

The true starting-point for the world's progress will never be reached by any nation as a whole. It exists and has been reached in the past as it will in the future by individuals scattered here and there in every nation. It is reached by those minds which insist on seeing conditions as they are, and which cannot confine their thoughts to their own kitchen, or to their own creed, or to their own nation. You will think I have in mind poets and philosophers, for these men take humanity as their subject, and deal in the general stuff of human nature. But the narrow spirit in which they often do this cuts down their influence to parish limits. I mean rather those men who in private life act out their thoughts and feelings as to the unity of human life; those same thoughts which the poets and philosophers have expressed in their plays, their sayings, and their visions. There have always been men who in their daily life have fulfilled those intimations and instincts which, if reduced to a statement, receive the names of poetry and religion. These men are the cart-horses of progress, they devote their lives to doing things which can only be justified or explained by the highest philosophy. They proceed as if all men were their brothers. These practical philanthropists go plodding on through each century and leave the bones of their character mingled with the soil of their civilization.

See how large the labors of such men look when seen in historic perceptive. They have changed the world's public opinion. They have molded the world's institutions into forms expressive of their will. I ask your attention to one of their achievements. We have one province of conduct in which the visions of the poets have been reduced to practice—yes, erected into a department of government—through the labors of the philanthropists. They have established the hospital and the reformatory; and these visible bastions of philosophy hold now a more unchallenged place in our civilization than the Sermon on the Mount on which they comment.

The truth which the philanthropists of all ages have felt is that the human family was a unit; and this truth, being as deep as human nature, can be expressed in every philosophy—even in the inverted utilitarianism now in vogue. The problem of how to treat insane people and criminals has been solved to this extent, that everyone agrees that nothing must be done to them which injures the survivors. That is the reason we do not kill them. It is unpleasant to have them about, and this unpleasantness can be cured only by our devotion to them. We must either help the wretched or we ourselves become degenerate. They have thus become a positive means of civilizing the modern world; for the instinct of self-preservation has led men to deal with this problem in the only practical way.

Put a Chinaman into your hospital and he will be cared for. You may lie awake at night drawing up reasons for doing something different with this disgusting Chinaman—who, somehow, is in the world and is thrown into your care, your hospital, your thought—but the machinery of your own being is so constructed that if you take any other course with him than that which you take with your own people, your institution will instantly lose its meaning; you would not have the face to beg money for its continuance in the following year. The logic of this, which, if you like, is the logic of self-protection under the illusion of self-sacrifice, is the logic which is at the bottom of all human progress. I dislike to express this idea in its meanest form; but I know there are some professors of political economy here, and I wish to be understood. The utility of hospitals is not to cure the sick. It is to teach mercy. The veneration for hospitals is not accorded to them because they cure the sick, but because they stand for love, and responsibility.

The appeal of physical suffering makes the strongest attack on our common humanity. Even zealots and sectaries are touched. The practice and custom of this kind of mercy have therefore become established, while other kinds of mercy which require more imagination are still in their infancy. But at the bottom of every fight for principle you will find the same sentiment of mercy. If you take a slate and pencil and follow out the precise reasons and consequences of the thing, you will always find that a practical and effective love for mankind is working out a practical self-sacrifice. The average man cannot do the sum, he does not follow the reasoning, but he knows the answer. The deed strikes into his soul with a mathematical impact, and he responds like a tuning-fork when its note is struck.

Everyone knows that self-sacrifice is a virtue. The child takes his nourishment from the tale of heroism as naturally as he takes milk. He feels that the deed was done for his sake. He adopts it: it is his own. The nations have always stolen their myths from one another, and claimed each other's heroes. It has required all the world's heroes to make the world's ear sensitive to new statements, illustrations and applications of the logic of progress. Yet their work has been so well done that all of us respond to the old truths in however new a form. Not France alone but all modern society owes a debt of gratitude to Zola for his rescue of Dreyfus. The whole world would have been degraded and set back, the whole world made less decent and habitable, but for those few Frenchmen who took their stand against corruption.

Now the future of civil society upon the earth depends upon the application to international politics of this familiar idea, which we see prefigured in our mythology, and monumentalized in our hospitals—the principle that what is done for one is done for all. When you say a thing is "right," you appeal to mankind. What you mean is that everyone is at stake. Your attack upon wrong amounts to saying that some one has been left out in the calculation. Both at home and abroad you are always pleading for mercy, and the plea gains such a wide response that some tyranny begins to totter, and its engines are turned upon you to get you to stop. This outcry against you is the measure of your effectiveness. If you imitate Zola and attack some nuisance in this town to-morrow, you will bring on every symptom and have every experience of the Dreyfus affair. The cost is the same, for cold looks are worse than imprisonment. The emancipation of

The Unity of Human Nature

the reformer is the same, for if a man can resist the influences of his townsfolk, if he can cut free from the tyranny of neighborhood gossip, the world has no terrors for him; there is no second inquisition. The public influence is the same, for every citizen of that town can thereafter look a town officer in the face with more self-respect. But not to townsmen, nor to neighboring towns, nor to Parisians is this force confined. It goes out in all directions, continuously. The man is in communication with the world. This impulse of communication with all men is at the bottom of every ambition. The injustice, cruelty, oppression in the world are all different forms of the same non-conductor, that prevents utterances, that stops messages, that strikes dumb the speaker and deafens the listener. You will find that it makes no difference whether the non-conductor be a selfish oligarchy, a military autocracy, or a commercial ring. The voice of humanity is stifled by corruption: and corruption is only an evil because it stifles men.

Try to raise a voice that shall be heard from here to Albany and watch what it is that comes forward to shut off the sound. It is not a German sergeant, nor a Russian officer of the precinct. It is a note from a friend of your father's offering you a place in his office. This is your warning from the secret police. Why, if any of you young gentlemen have a mind to make himself heard a mile off, you must make a bonfire of your reputations and a close enemy of most men who wish you well.

And what will you get in return? Well, if I must for the benefit of the economist, charge you with some selfish gain, I will say that you get the satisfaction of having been heard, and that this is the whole possible scope of human ambition.

When I was asked to make this address, I wondered what I had to say to you boys who are graduating. And I think I have one thing to say. If you wish to be useful, never take a course that will silence you. Refuse to learn anything that you cannot proclaim. Refuse to accept anything that implies collusion, whether it be a clerkship or a curacy, a legal fee or a post in a university. Retain the power of speech, no matter what other power you lose. If you can take this course, and in so far as you take it, you will bless this country. In so far as you depart from this course, you become dampers, mutes, and hooded executioners. As for your own private character, it will be preserved by such a course. Crime you cannot commit, for crime gags you. Collusion with any abuse gags you. As a practical matter a mere failure to speak out upon occasions where no opinion is asked or expected of you, and when the utterance of an uncalled-for suspicion is odious, will often hold you to a concurrence in palpable iniquity. It will bind and gag you and lay you dumb and in shackles like the veriest serf in Russia. I give you this one rule of conduct. Do what you will, but speak out always. Be shunned, be hated, be ridiculed, be scared, be in doubt, but don't be gagged.

The choice of Hercules was made when Hercules was a lad. It cannot be made late in life. It will perhaps come for each one of you within the next eighteen months. I have seen ten years of young men who rush out into the world with their messages, and when they find how deaf the world is, they think they must save their strength and wait. They believe that after a while they will be able to get up on some little eminence from which they can make themselves heard. "In a few years," reasons one of them, "I shall have gained a standing, and then I will use my power for good." Next year comes and with it a strange discovery. The man has lost his horizon of thought. His ambition has evaporated; he has nothing to say. The great occasion that was to have let him loose on society was some little occasion that nobody saw, some moment in which he decided to obtain a standing. The great battle of a lifetime has been fought and lost over a silent scruple. But for this, the man might, within a few years, have spoken to the nation with the voice of an archangel. What was he waiting for? Did he think that the laws of nature were to be changed for him? Did he thing that a "notice of trial" would be served on him? Or that some spirit would stand at his elbow and say, "Now's your time?" The time of trial is always. Now is the appointed time. And the compensation for beginning at once is that your voice carries at once. You do not

The Unity of Human Nature

need a standing. It would not help you. Within less time than you can see it, you will have been heard. The air is filled with sounding-boards and the echoes are flying. It is ten to one that you have but to lift your voice to be heard in California, and that from where you stand. A bold plunge will teach you that the visions of the unity of human nature which the poets have sung, were not the fictions of their imagination, but a record of what they saw. Deal with the world, and you will discover their reality. Speak to the world, and you will hear their echo.

Social and business prominence look like advantages, and so they are if you want money. But if you want moral influence you may bless God you have not got them. They are the payment with which the world subsidizes men to keep quiet, and there is no subtilty or cunning by which you can get them without paying in silence. This is the great law of humanity, that has existed since history began, and will last while man lasts—evil, selfishness, and silence are one thing.

The world is learning, largely through American experience, that freedom in the form of government is no guarantee against abuse, tyranny, cruelty, and greed. The old sufferings, the old passions are in full blast among us. What, then, are the advantages of self-government? The chief advantage is that self-government enables a man in his youth, in his own town, within the radius of his first public interests, to fight the important battle of his life while his powers are at their strongest, and the powers of oppression are at their weakest. If a man acquires the power of speech here, if he says what he means now, if he makes his point and dominates his surroundings at once, his voice will, as a matter of fact, be heard instantly in a very wide radius. And so he walks up into a new sphere and begins to accomplish greater things. He does this through the very force of his insistence on the importance of small things. The reason for his graduation is not far to seek. A man cannot reach the hearts of his townsfolk, without using the whole apparatus of the world of thought. He cannot tell or act the truth in his own town without enlisting every power for truth, and setting in vibration the cords that knit that town into the world's history. He is forced to find and strike the same note which he would use on some great occasion when speaking for all mankind. A man who has won a town-fight is a veteran, and our country to-day is full of these young men. To-morrow their force will show in national politics, and in that moment the fate of the Malay, the food of the Russian prisoner, the civilization of South Africa, and the future of Japan will be seen to have been in issue. These world problems are now being settled in the contest over the town-pump in a western village. I think it likely that the next thirty years will reveal the recuperative power of American institutions. One of you young men may easily become a reform President, and be carried into office and held in office by the force of that private opinion which is now being sown broadcast throughout the country by just such men as yourselves. You will concede the utility of such a President. Yet it would not be the man but the masses behind him that did his work.

Democracy thus lets character loose upon society and shows us that in the realm of natural law there is nothing either small or great: and this is the chief value of democracy. In America the young man meets the struggle between good and evil in the easiest form in which it was ever laid before men. The cruelties of interest and of custom have with us no artificial assistance from caste, creed, race prejudice. Our frame of government is drawn in close accordance with the laws of nature. By our documents we are dedicated to mankind; and hence it is that we can so easily feel the pulse of the world and lay our hand on the living organism of humanity.

[1910]

The Doctrine of Non-Resistance*

A dogma is a phrase that condenses much thought. It is a short way of stating a great truth, and is supposed to recall that truth to the mind. Like a talisman it is to be repeated. Open sesame—and some great mystery of life is unlocked.

A dogma is like a key to a map, a thread to a labyrinth. It is all that some man has brought back from a spiritual exaltation in which he has had a vision of how the world is made; and he repeats it and teaches it as a digest of his vision, a short and handy summary and elixir by which he, and as he thinks anyone else, can go back into his exaltation and see the truth. To him the words seem universally true—true at all times and in any aspect. Indeed, all experience, all thought, all conduct seem to him to be made up of mere illustrations, proofs, and reminiscences of the dogma.

It is probable that all the dogmas were originally shots at the same truth, nets cast over the same truth, digests of the same vision. There is no other way of accounting for their power. If

*This was an address which I delivered before the International Metaphysical League eight or nine years ago. [Chapman included this note when the essay was reprinted in 1910.]

the doctrine of the Trinity signified no more than what I can see in it, it would never have been regarded as important. Unless the words "Salvation by Grace" had at one time stood for the most powerful conviction of the most holy minds, we should never have heard the phrase. Our nearest way to come at the meaning of such things is to guess that the dogmas are the dress our own thought might have worn, had we lived in times when they arose. We must translate our best selves back into the past in order to understand the phrases.

Of course, these dogmas, like our own dogmas, are no sooner uttered than they change. Somebody traduces them, or expounds them, or founds a sect or a prosecution upon them. Then comes a new vision and a new digest. And so the controversy goes rolling down through the centuries, changing its forms but not its substance. And it has rolled down to us, and we are asking the question, "What is truth?" as eagerly, as sincerely, and as patiently as we may.

Truth is a state of mind. All of us have known it and have known the loss of it. We enter it unconsciously; we pass out of it before we are aware. It comes and goes like a searchlight from an unknown source. At one moment we see all things clearly, at the next we are fighting a fog. At one moment we are as weak as rags, at the next we are in contact with some explaining power that courses through us, making us feel like electrical conductors, or the agents of universal will. In the language of Christ these latter feelings are moments of "faith"; and faith is one of the very few words which he used a great many times in just the same sense, as a name for a certain kind of experience. He did not define the word, but he seems to have given it a specific meaning.

The state of mind in which Christ lived is the truth he taught. How he reached that state of mind we do not know; how he maintained it, and what it is, he spent the last two years of his life in expressing. Whatever he was saying or doing, he was always conveying the same truth—the whole of it. It was never twice alike and yet it was always the same; even when he spoke very few words, as to Pilate "Thou sayest it," or to Peter "Feed my sheep"; or when he said nothing, but wrote on the ground. He not only expressed this truth because he could not help expressing it, but because he wished and strove to express it. His teaching, his parables, his sayings showed that he spared no pains to think of illustrations and suggestions; he used every device of speech to make his thought carry.

Take his directest words: "Thou shalt love the Lord thy God"; "Love your enemies." One might call these things descriptions of his own state of mind. Or take his philosophical remarks. They are not merely statements as to what truth is; but hints as to how it must be sought, how the state of mind can be entered into and in what it consists. "Whosoever shall lose his life shall preserve it." "That which cometh out of the mouth, this defileth a man." Or more prosaically still. "If any man shall do his will, he shall know of the doctrine." To this class belongs the expression "Resist not evil."

The parables are little anecdotes which serve to remind the hearer of his own moments of tenderness and self-sacrifice. The Lost Sheep, the Prodigal Son, the Good Samaritan, the Repentant Sinner, are illustrations of Christ's way of feeling toward human nature. They are less powerful than his words and acts, because no constructed thing has the power of a real thing. The reply of the Greek woman who besought Christ to cure her daughter, "Yes, Lord, yet the dogs under the table eat of the children's crumbs," is one of the most affecting things in the New Testament. It is more powerful than the tale of the Prodigal Son. But you will see that if the Prodigal's father had been a real father, and the Greek mother had been a personage in a parable, the power would have been the other way.

And so it is that Christ's most powerful means of conveying his thought was neither by his preaching nor by his parables; but by what he himself said and did incidentally. This expressed his doctrine because his state of feeling was his doctrine. The things Christ did by himself and the words he said to himself, these things are Christianity—his washing the disciples' feet, "Forgive them, for they know not what they do," his crucifixion.

I have recalled all these sayings and acts of Christ almost at random. They seem to me to be equivalent one to another as a thousand is equivalent to a thousand. They are all messages sent out by the same man in the same state of feeling. If he had lived longer, there would have been more of them. If you should summarize them all into a philosophy and then reduce that philosophy to a phrase, you would have another dogma.

The reason I called this lecture Non-resistance instead of using some more general religious title, is that I happened to be led into re-examining the meaning of Christ's sayings through his phrase "Resist not evil; but overcome evil with good." It came about in the course of many struggles over practical reforms. I had not the smallest religious or theoretical bias in entering the field of politics. Here were certain actual cruelties, injurious things done by particular men, in plain sight. They ought to be stopped.

The question is how to do it. First you go to the wrongdoers and beg them to stop, and they will not stop. Then to the officials in authority over them, with the same result. "Remove these officials" is now your conclusion, and you go and join the party that keeps them in power; for you intend to induce that party to change them. You now engage in infinitely long, exhausting struggles with the elements of wickedness, which seem to be the real cause and support of those injuries which you are trying to stop. You make no headway; you find you are wasting force; you are fighting at a disadvantage; all your energies are exhausted in antagonism. It occurs to you to join the other party, and induce that party to advocate a positive good, whereby the people may be appealed to and the iniquities voted down. But your trouble here begins afresh, for it seems as hard to induce the "outs" to make a square attack on the evil as it is to get the "ins" to desist from doing the evil. Your struggle, your antagonism, your waste of energy continues. At last you leave the outs and form a new party, a reform party of your own. Merciful heavens! neither will this new party attack wickedness. Your mind, your thought, your time is still taken up in resist-

The Doctrine of Non-Resistance

ing the influences which your old enemies are bringing to bear upon your new friends.

I had got as far as this in the experience and had come to see plainly that there was somewhere a mistake in my method. It was a mistake to try to induce others to act. The thing to do was to act myself, alone and directly, without waiting for help. I should thus at least be able to do what I knew to be right; and perhaps this was the strongest appeal I could make to anyone. The thing to do was to run independent candidates and ask the public to support good men. Then there occurred to me the phrase, "Resist not evil," and the phrase seemed to explain the experience.

What had I been doing all these years but wrangling over evil? I had a system that pitted me in a ring against certain agencies of corruption and led to unending antagonism. The phrase not only explained what was wrong with the whole system, but what was wrong with every human contact that occurred under it. The more you thought of it, the truer it seemed. It was not merely true of politics, it was true of all human intercourse. The politics of New York bore the same sort of relation to this truth that a kodak does to the laws of optics. Our politics were a mere illustration of it. The phrase seemed to explain everything either wrong or mistaken that I had ever done in my life. To meet selfishness with selfishness, anger with anger, irritation with irritation, that was the harm. But the saying was not exhausted yet. The phrase passed over into physiology and showed how to cure a cramp in a muscle or stop a headache. It was true as religion, true as pathology, and true as to everything between them. I felt as a modern mathematician might feel, who should find inscribed in an Egyptian temple a mathematical formula which not only included all he knew, but showed that all he knew was a mere stumbling comment on the ancient science.

What mind was it that walked the earth and put the sum of wisdom into three words? By what process was it done? The impersonal precision and calm of the statement give it the quality of geometry, and yet it expresses nothing but human feeling. I suppose that Christ arrived at the remark by simple introspection. The impulse which he felt in himself to oppose evil with evil—he puts his finger on that impulse as the crucial danger. There is in the phrase an extreme care, as if he were explaining a mechanism. He seems to be saying "If you wish to open the door, you must lift the latch before you pull the handle. If you wish to do good, you must resist evil with good, not with evil."

It is the same with his other sayings. They are almost dry, they are so accurate. "Whosoever looketh on a woman to lust after her hath committed adultery with her already in his heart"; the analysis of emotion could hardly be carried farther. "How hard it is for them that trust in riches to enter into the Kingdom of God"; here is neither exaggeration nor epigram. "Thy faith hath made thee whole"; a statement of fact. "Knock and it shall be opened unto you"; this is the summary of Christ's whole life down to the time his teaching began. He had knocked and it had been opened to him. He had wished to make men better, and inasmuch as he wished it harder than anyone else before or since has wished it, he got farther than anyone toward an understanding of how to do it. The effectiveness of his thought has been due to its coherence. He was able to draw the sky together over any subject till all the light fell on one point. Then he said what he saw. Every question was shown to break up into the same crystals if subjected to the same pressure. Nor does his influence upon the world present any anomaly. It is entirely due to ordinary causes. Every man's influence depends upon the depth of his will; for this determines his power of concentration. The controlled force that could contract Christ's own mind to so small a focus, brings down to the same focus other minds of less coherence than his. This is will; this is leadership; this is power.

Yet in spite of his will there were plenty of things that Christ himself could not do, as, for instance, change the world at once, or change it at all except through the slow process of personal influence. He could not heal people who had no faith, or get followers except by going into the highways and hedges after them. And his whole life is as valuable in showing what cannot be done, as in showing what can be done. If you love your fel-

The Doctrine of Non-Resistance

low-men and wish to benefit them, you will find that the ways in which it is possible to do this are not many. You can do harm in many ways, good only in one.

The world is full of people who want to do good, and men are constantly re-discovering Christ. This intelligence, superior to our own, possesses and utilizes us. There is always more danger of his influence being perverted than of its dying out; for as men begin to discover the scope and horizon of his thought they are tempted to becloud it with commentary. They wish to say what he meant, whereas he has said it himself. We think to explain something whose value is that it explains us. If we understood him, very likely we should say nothing.

The mistake Christians make is that they strive to follow Christ as a gnat follows a candle. No man ought to follow Christ in this way. A man ought to follow truth, and when he does this, he will find that, as he gropes his way through life, most of the light that falls on the path in front of him, and moves as he moves, comes from the mind of Christ. But if one is to learn from that mind one must take it as a lens through which to view truth; not as truth itself. We do not look at a lens, but through it.

There are moments in each of our lives when all the things that Christ said seem clear, sensible, relevant. The use of his sayings is to remind us of these moments and carry us back into them. The danger of his sayings is lest we rely upon them as final truth. They are no more truth than the chemical equivalents for food are food, or than certain symbols of dynamics are the power of Niagara. At those moments when the real Niagara is upon us we must keep our minds bent on how to do good to our fellow-men; not the partial good of material benevolence, but the highest good we know. The thoughts and habits we thus form and work out, painfully plotting over them, revising, renewing, remodeling them, become our personal church. This is our own religion, this is our clue to truth, this is the avenue through which we may pass back to truth and possess it. No other cord will hold except the one a man has woven himself. No other key will serve except the one a man has forged himself.

Christ was able to hold a prism perfectly still in his hand so as to dissolve a ray of light into its elements. Every time he speaks, he splits open humanity, as a man might crack a nut and show the kernel. The force of human feeling behind these sayings can be measured only by their accomplishments. They have been re-arranging and overturning human society ever since. By this most unlikely means of quiet demonstration in word and deed, did he unlock this gigantic power. The bare fragments of his talk open the sluices of our minds; they overwhelm and re-create. That was his method. The truth which he conveyed with such metaphysical accuracy lives now in the living. Very likely we cannot express it in dogmas, for such intellect as it takes to utter a dogma is not in us. But we need have no fear for our power of expressing it. It is enough for us to see truth; for if we see it, everything we do will express it.

[1900]

William James

None of us will ever see a man like William James again: there is no doubt about that. And yet it is hard to state what it was in him that gave him either his charm or his power, what it was that penetrated and influenced us, what it is that we lack and feel the need of, now that he has so unexpectedly and incredibly died. I always thought that William James would continue forever; and I relied upon his sanctity as if it were sunlight.

I should not have been abashed at being discovered in some mean action by William James; because I should have felt that he would understand and make allowances. The abstract and sublime quality of his nature was always enough for two; and I confess to having always trespassed upon him and treated him with impertinence, without gloves, without reserve, without ordinary, decent concern for the sentiments and weaknesses of human character. Knowing nothing about philosophy, and having the dimmest notions as to what James's books might contain, I used occasionally to write and speak to him about his specialties in a tone of fierce contempt; and never failed to elicit from him in reply the most spontaneous and celestial gayety. Certainly he was a wonderful man.

He was so devoid of selfish aim or small personal feeling that your shafts might pierce, but could never wound him. You could not "diminish one dowle that's in his plume." Where he walked, nothing could touch him; and he enjoyed the Emersonian immunity of remaining triumphant even after he had been vanquished. The reason was, as it seems to me, that what the man really meant was always something indestructible and persistent; and that he knew this inwardly. He had not the gift of expression, but rather the gift of suggestion. He said things which meant one thing to him and something else to the reader or listener. His mind was never quite in focus, and there was always something left over after each discharge of the battery, something which now became the beginning of a new thought. When he found out his mistake or defect of expression, when he came to see that he had not said quite what he meant, he was the first to proclaim it, and to move on to a new position, a new misstatement of the same truth,—a new, debonair apperception, clothed in non-conclusive and suggestive figures of speech.

How many men have put their shoulders out of joint in striking at the phantasms which James projected upon the air! James was always in the right, because what he meant was true. The only article of his which I ever read with proper attention was "The Will to Believe," a thing that exasperated me greatly until I began to see, or to think I saw, what James meant, and at the same time to acknowledge to myself that he had said something quite different. I hazard this idea about James as one might hazard an idea about astronomy, fully aware that it may be very foolish.

In private life and conversation there was the same radiation of thought about him. The center and focus of his thought fell within his nature, but not within his intellect. You were thus played upon by a logic which was not the logic of intellect, but a far deeper thing, limpid and clear in itself, confused and refractory only when you tried to deal with it intellectually. You must take any fragment of such a man by itself, for his whole meaning is in the fragment. If you try to piece the bits together, you will endanger their meaning. In general talk on life, literature, and politics James was always throwing off sparks that were cognate only in this, that they came from the same central fire in him. It was easy to differ from him; it was easy to go home thinking that James had talked the most arrant rubbish, and that no educated man had a right to be so ignorant of the first principles of thought and of the foundations of human society. Yet it was impossible not to be morally elevated by the smallest contact with William James. A refining, purgatorial influence came out of him.

I believe that in his youth, James dedicated himself to the glory of God and the advancement of Truth, in the same spirit that a young knight goes to seek the Grail, or a young military hero dreams of laying down his life for his country. What his early leanings towards philosophy or his natural talent for it may have been, I do not know; but I feel as if he had first taken up philosophy out of a sense of duty,—the old Puritanical impulse,—in his case illumined, however, with a humor and genius not at all of the Puritan type. He adopted philosophy as his lance and buckler,—psychology, it was called in his day,—and it proved to be as good as the next thing,—as pliable as poetry or fiction or politics or law would have been,—or anything else that he might have adopted as a vehicle through which his nature could work upon society.

He, himself, was all perfected from the beginning, a selfless angel. It is this quality of angelic unselfishness which gives the power to his work. There may be some branches of human study—mechanics perhaps—where the personal spirit of the investigator does not affect the result; but philosophy is not one of them. Philosophy is a personal vehicle; and every man makes his own, and through it he says what he has to say. It is all personal: it is all human: it is all non-reducible to science, and incapable of being either repeated or continued by another man.

Now James was an illuminating ray, a dissolvent force. He looked freshly at life, and read books freshly. What he had to say about them was not entirely articulated, but was always spontaneous. He seemed to me to have too high an opinion of everything. The last book he had read was always "a great book"; the last person he had talked with, a wonderful being. If I may judge from my own standpoint, I should say that James saw too much good in everything, and felt towards everything a too indiscriminating approval. He was always classing things up into places they didn't belong and couldn't remain in.

Of course, we know that Criticism is proverbially an odious thing; it seems to deal only in shadows,—it acknowledges only varying shades of badness in everything. And we know, too, that Truth is light; Truth cannot be expressed in shadow, except by some subtle art which proclaims the shadow-part to be the lie, and the non-expressed part to be the truth. And it is easy to look upon the whole realm of Criticism and see in it nothing but a science which concerns itself with the accurate statement of lies. Such, in effect, it is in the hands of most of its adepts. Now James's weakness as a critic was somehow connected with the peculiar nature of his mind, which lived in a consciousness of light. The fact is that James was non-critical, and therefore divine. He was forever hovering, and never could alight; and this is a quality of truth and a quality of genius.

The great religious impulse at the back of all his work, and which pierces through at every point, never became expressed in conclusive literary form, or in dogmatic utterance. It never became formulated in his own mind into a statable belief. And yet it controlled his whole life and mind, and accomplished a great work in the world. The spirit of a priest was in him,—in his books and in his private conversation. He was a sage, and a holy man; and everybody put off his shoes before him. And yet in spite of this,—in conjunction with this, he was a sportive, wayward, Gothic sort of spirit, who was apt, on meeting a friend, to burst into foolery, and whose wit was always three parts poetry. Indeed his humor was as penetrating as his seriousness. Both of these two sides of James's nature—the side that made a direct religious appeal, and the side that made a veiled religious appeal—became rapidly intensified during his later years; so that, had the process continued much longer, the mere sight of him must have moved beholders to amend their lives.

I happened to be at Oxford at one of his lectures in 1908; and it was remarkable to see the reverence which that very unrevering class of men—the University dons—evinced towards James, largely on account of his appearance and personality. The fame of him went abroad, and the Sanhedrim attended. A quite distinguished, and very fussy scholar, a member of the old guard of Nil-admirari Cultivation,—who would have sniffed nervously if he had met Moses—told me that he had gone to a lecture of James's, "though the place was so crowded, and stank so that he had to come away immediately."—"But," he added, "he certainly has the face of a sage."

There was, in spite of his playfulness, a deep sadness about James. You felt that he had just stepped out of this sadness in order to meet you, and was to go back into it the moment you left him. It may be that sadness inheres in some kinds of profoundly religious characters,—in dedicated persons who have renounced all, and are constantly hoping, thinking, acting, and (in the typical case) praying for humanity. Lincoln was sad, and Tolstoi was sad, and many sensitive people, who view the world as it is, and desire nothing for themselves except to become of use to others, and to become agents in the spread of truth and happiness,—such people are often sad. It has sometimes crossed my mind that James wanted to be a poet and an artist, and that there lay in him, beneath the ocean of metaphysics, a lost Atlantis of the fine arts; that he really hated philosophy and all its works, and pursued them only as Hercules might spin, or as a prince in a fairy tale might sort seeds for an evil dragon, or as anyone might patiently do some careful work for which he had no aptitude. It would seem most natural, if this were the case between James and the metaphysical sciences; for what is there in these studies that can drench and satisfy a tingling mercurial being who loves to live on the surface, as well as in the depths of life? Thus we reason, forgetting that the mysteries of temperament are deeper than the mysteries of occupation. If James had

had the career of Molière, he would still have been sad. He was a victim of divine visitation: the Searching Spirit would have winnowed him in the same manner, no matter what avocation he might have followed.

The world watched James as he pursued through life his search for religious truth; the world watched him, and often gently laughed at him, asking, "When will James arise and fly? When will 'he take the wings of the morning, and dwell in the uttermost parts of the sea'?" And in the meantime, James was there already. Those were the very places that he was living in. Through all the difficulties of polyglot metaphysics and of modern psychology he waded for years, lecturing and writing and existing,—and creating for himself a public which came to see in him only the saint and the sage, which felt only the religious truth which James was in search of, yet could never quite grasp in his hand. This very truth constantly shone out through him,—shone, as it were, straight through his waistcoat,—and distributed itself to everyone in the drawing-room, or in the lecture-hall where he sat. Here was the familiar paradox, the old parable, the psychological puzzle of the world. "But what went ye out for to see?" In the very moment that the world is deciding that a man was no prophet and had nothing to say, in that very moment perhaps is his work perfected, and he himself is gathered to his fathers, after having been a lamp to his own generation, and an inspiration to those who came after.

[1910]

Dr. Horace Howard Furness

Dr. Furness was at the time of his death the most famous of American scholars. The sixteen great volumes of his Variorum Shakespeare are like the Fondacio dei Tedeschi at Venice,—a casket and a monument, a thing of beauty and a symbol of ancient wealth.

In one of his prefaces Dr. Furness says that every textual variant of the volume in question has been thrice verified by himself. These textual variants or alternate readings are the ashes of the various texts that have successively been evolved and destroyed by one and another of Shakespeare's editors since the earliest times; and these ashes are preserved, lest perchance a little scrap of gold should somewhere be left among them, or lest there should lurk in them some gleam of the life of that phoenix that flew forth out of them.

But the labor of endless textual detail is only one feature of Dr. Furness's work on Shakespeare's monument. The other sides of his work are less dreadful to think of. His aim was to bring the substance of all the books ever written about Shakespeare into the compass of a single edition. Any other man would have attacked his work like a beaver. Dr. Furness attacked it like a bee. His sunny disposition turned the gigantic work into pleasure. And here a strange fact may be perceived—that Dr. Furness ended by weaving his own character and personality into this edition as completely as if he had been writing his memoirs, or making a portrait of himself for posterity. Furness's notes and glossaries abound in that playful tenderness which I feel sure was the characteristic quality of Shakespeare himself. I am certain that an unwillingness to hurt anyone's feelings was the most noticeable quality in Shakespeare, and that this is why Shakespeare was so often called "gentle" by his contemporaries. (Imagine a stage-manager who should be nicknamed "gentle" to-day!)

If, as I just said, Dr. Furness has written himself into these volumes, it is because in dealing with the Shakespeare legends he only takes what he loves, and he only loves thyme and sweetwilliam. If a subject displeases him, he drops it. For instance, he cannot bear to speak ill of such a good Elizabethan as John Payne Collier; and he, therefore, frankly says that no discussion of the Collier forgery question can be looked for from him. This is not what is called scholarship; but it is something better than scholarship, it is character, it is temperament, it is vitality.

No great scholar has ever written such a good commentary on Shakespeare as Dr. Furness has written; because all great scholars are apt to become bores. It is really their duty and their destiny to be bores. Even A.C. Bradley, the latest and greatest of Shakespearian scholars, is just a little, slightly a bore. The note of virtuosity is in him. Dr. Furness was really engaged in arranging, condensing, and transcribing the things that he thought vital in Shakespeare's literary history. He was one kind of a scholar; but he belonged to that type and species of scholarship of which Bishop Percy and Walter Scott are examples, the species to whom literature is food and drink. To some modern scholars, literature is a dead body, or at least a subject for vivisection—never a live animal to be stroked and talked to, befriended, lived with, laughed and cried over.

Furness's tone about his own views is so modest that he almost seems to have no views of his own; and when he suggests an idea of his own, he barely hazards it, and that in the fewest words. What great scholar ever did the like? Dr. Furness collects all the bones and tidbits from three hundred years of Shakespearian controversy; and having laid them before you, scampers away with a jest. The result is that he has written enchanting commentaries which frame Shakespeare with a genial sort of foolery that is near kin to Shakespeare's own spirit.

This Variorum Edition will cause many old Shakespeariana to go out of print. The positive results of many a great commentator's life may be embodied in an improved text; and the wagonloads of disquisition which at first were essential, soon become superfluous through their very success. The same reasoning holds good in regard to the theories which course like dolphins in Shakespeare's wake, theories as to the chronology of the plays, theories as to the sources of their plots, and the metaphysics of their characters. A brochure upon any such topic will in a few years shrink and dry up, till it can be carried in a mere footnote. Indeed, any idea must be quite monumental at the beginning of its career, in order that posterity shall afford it more than an asterisk.

The notes and disquisitions in the Variorum Edition give you all you are ever likely to want of a host of old worthies and worthiesses who strutted their little day, and penned with quill pens and steel pens their various comments. I love the race of men who write notes on great books, whether on Dante or on Shakespeare. They collect miscellaneous information and they chatter like happy magpies. They keep literature alive, like Darwin's earthworms, by creeping down out of sight and bringing new soil to the top. Without them some poets would be incomprehensible within a few decades after death. Dante would be unread to-day, Chaucer and Shakespeare would be almost gone, and Byron would be on the road to oblivion. To put all the Shakespeare chatterers into one great aviary, to tame them, docket them, assign them their perches and index them—this was the work of Dr. Furness's life. The Variorum is really a Shakespeare library; and no private person has need to encumber his shelves with more authorities than this edition supplies. If a man wants to make a beast of himself, let him go to a public library.

My acquaintance with Dr. Furness was slight, or rather, I should say, it was short, and did not occur till 1912, when he was in his seventy-ninth year. But the man himself casts back such a light on his books, and his books now begin to cast forward such a light on the man, that his image is very clear in my mind. It is the image of the perfect scholar, and of the great gentleman, through whom there yet shines a crystal idea of something nobler than either. He was all his life a man of various social activities and of great influence; and this contact with life gave him a robustness and rotundity of nature which literary men often lack.

He certainly was the most picturesque old gentleman that I have ever known. He was short and stout—his head, with its large dome, was fringed with the most brilliant white hair—immaculate, gleaming hair. His gold eyeglasses, which were very transparent and which magnified the gray eyes behind them, his elegant, delicate silver ear-trumpet—(more like some elfin horn, or the ornament of a fairy king or goblin herald, than a necessary instrument), that horn which was always at hand, always being adjusted to receive good news from the guest—his wonderful neatness and trimness—as if his waistcoat and watchchain had been burnished upon him—as if his clothes were made of bronze, or as if he were a drawing by Ingres—all these things, as well as the smiling trustfulness (like that of a good child) with which he welcomed everyone, took him out of the actual. You could not believe that he was true. He was as a picture, or as a character of the imagination. Of course he really did belong to a familiar epoch; but somehow his deafness had isolated him and surrounded him with an invisible hothouse. There was a bloom upon him; he radiated a sort of heaven-sent bonhomie. I am sure that if I had seen him in a railroad station without knowing who he was, I should have followed him home, tracked him to his habitat, so as to assure myself that he was an earthborn creature.

Think of such a man's having lived in the America of to-day!

He might have come out of London in 1811; he might have lived in Edinburgh in 1830. He was like Charles Lamb; he seemed to be clad in knee-breeches; he was all leisure, all literature, all tenderness for the feelings of others. I am sure that this quality of hating to hurt anyone's feelings, of avoiding the unpleasant, must somewhere, somehow have run into vice with Dr. Furness. It is wrong to be so tender as he was.

Dr. Furness, as everyone knows, was deaf—so very deaf that one had to speak into his silver ear-trumpet and speak quite loudly in order to reach him. Yet his deafness never separated him from the rest of society, but on the contrary it joined him to others. His expression of perfect benevolence and perfect accord, as he surveyed the dinner-table, his smile of expectation as he caught your eye, gave you something to say. You could not be dumb in his presence. In fact, his deafness had the very opposite influence to that which deafness usually has: it drew you out. He elicited extravagant sallies; he invited foolishness: and when foolishness came, he welcomed it as the Father in the parable welcomed the Prodigal. One knew all the while that somewhere in the middle of all this gayety there lay a great renunciation. This power to give and take innocent pleasure is always bought with a great price. A big lump sum has been paid down at some time in the past, so great that the interest of it supports the donor forever after; he is care-free.

Dr. Furness had cunning ways, he did cunning things; but they were always very clever. He himself was never deceived for a moment. He understood his drolleries well enough. When, for instance, I asked him why it was, or why he thought it was, that Fanny Kemble had singled out just him as the person to whom she should give Shakespeare's gloves—he assumed the attitude of the ingénue in old English comedy—put his knuckles to his lips, looked archly at the ceiling, bent his head from side to side—"I don't know, I don't know." A lifelong familiarity with old English stage businesses had given him quite a battery of odd little gestures and tones of voice, which were as natural to him as they were unexpected by everyone else.

Dr. Furness had habits of a clockwork regularity. He rose at a certain hour, whatever it was, to the minute, and appeared at breakfast, which was a stately and sumptuous meal, long, luxurious, and social. Then he suddenly disappeared, and I don't know what he did for several hours. He performed his Shakespearian work in the middle of the night. After sitting up cracking jokes, or reading aloud, till twelve or one, he dismissed everyone and sat down to work till cock-crow. His library was of that sort which is added to the house as a unity—is lighted from the top and surrounded inside with a balcony. The room was full of memorials, pictures, and photographs, and was lined with all the books about Shakespeare, I suppose, in the world. In a small vault or inner sanctuary beyond, a fire-proof holy of holies, he kept his first editions. He had all the folios and a great many of the quartos. (I'm not sure that it is possible to have them all.) Here were kept other treasures more remarkable still—namely, fragments of Shakespeare's mulberry tree, and a pair of gloves which originally belonged to Shakespeare's theatrical properties, and which, after the playwright's decease, were shipped to Avon from London together with the rest of his belongings. These gloves are perhaps the most precious personal relic in the world. I do not know what doubts scholars may throw on their authenticity; but their history is well known and forms a part of the annals of the British stage. At any rate, I felt in looking on them an overwhelming belief in them—a pang of belief, such as no other personal relic ever gave me.

I cannot say that I always agree with Dr. Furness's views upon Shakespeare's characters. This is a subject upon which the clodhopper has rights of opinion; and some of Dr. Furness's theses seem to me to reflect his own temperament too closely—as, for instance, his views on the love affair between Anthony and Cleopatra. I must confess that his opinions here seem to me to be misjudged and even fantastic. Dr. Furness's romanticism has misled him. It is himself, [not Anthony, and not Shakespeare] that the seraphic Doctor has depicted in his rhapsodical preface to his play. And yet this same enthusiasm which, in this case, betrays Dr. Furness is the pervading cause of his charm. Dr. Furness is never really interested in anything except the poetic kernel of Shakespeare. He deals with the other parts because they must be dealt with. But the reason for all the husk is not to be found in the husk; the reason lies in the poetry. Furness never forgets this; he is in love all the time. He had the sort of adoration for Shakespeare that a schoolboy has for an elder brother. When this quality gets into a book of any sort, the book becomes happy and vigorous. "Isn't he a glorious fellow? Did you ever hear anything like him?" This is what Furness seems to be constantly saying.

Such is the general nature of Dr. Furness's contributions to Shakespeare's criticism. They sound so small and are so tremendous. For I suppose that the sunlight hidden everywhere in these big yellow volumes is enough to warm the earth. It will surely affect the disposition of all future commentators; and even the philologist, the comparative grammarian, the Indo-Germanic person may be softened, tinged, sweetened, and made into something more nearly resembling a human being, through contact with the unscientific, non-conclusive intellect of Horace Howard Furness.

∾

A short time before his death, Dr. Furness sent me a copy of his Phi Beta Kappa address entitled, "Shakespeare, or What You Will"; and in thanking him for it I sent him the verses printed below, which thus became the occasion of this paper. His death fell like a curtain, unexpectedly, without illness, without premonitory old age; and, as it fell, it left him in our imagination just as he had always appeared, standing in a sort of radiance.

"Yes, I have seen the wreath of woven flowers
   That in your garden (which is Shakespeare's mind)
Have blossomed freshly through the dewy hours,
   And which the deaf, old gardener smiled to find.

"Laughed as he found them—saved and wound and gave them:
    (The richest trophy that his life could bring),
Shakespeare's they are, and were, and he shall have them
    Forever as a fragrant offering.

"So, on thy bier, old servant, tried and tender,
    Some loving hand may lay a paler sheaf;
For none but Shakespeare might thy crimson render,
    Or match in words the greenness of thy leaf."

[1912]

Julia Ward Howe

The great Doctor Howe, whose figure towers over little Boston, was a man in middle life, and was well understood by Europe and America to be one of the world's wise men, when he married a New York girl of remarkable beauty, wit and wealth. This was in the year 1843. It made little difference to Dr. Howe where he lived, or what circle he moved in; but when he threw in his fortunes with the anti-slavery outcasts and Beacon Street looked askance at him, it made this difference to his wife, that she never really became a Bostonian. She lived, however, to become one of the best known personalities in the town, and to have a little court of her own. There was something about her which attracted individuals of all conditions, from foreign patriots,—the residuaries of Dr. Howe's revolutionary interests,—to the most modern representatives of every social reform. Her own people had been bankers, with harps and marble statues in their salons. Singing, and Italian lessons, and the provincial splendors of early New York had been hers; and after her marriage with Dr. Howe, she had traveled with him abroad and had seen many of the celebrities of Europe at a time when genius was in bloom there.

Apart from all this, she was in herself a daughter of the great liberal epoch of the nineteenth century which produced Bright, Garrison, Garibaldi and a whole race of lesser social missionaries who felt that they were marching to music, and who never doubted that clouds would break and truth triumph in the end,—men and women whose idealism and whose belief in the destinies of mankind bound them into a sort of brotherhood in world politics. She had, at any rate, lived among the heroes of her time, and she retained to the end a bigness and heroic outlook upon life which belonged to the epoch of her youth. Furthermore she was a poetess. In early married life she published a volume or two of verse, which were read and admired by the world of American letters, and the luster of which never quite left her. Neither she nor her circle ever forgot that there were laurels on her brow.

It must be remembered also that she continued in her own person the traditions of the Transcendentalists, whose school of thought became submerged in the welter of the anti-slavery struggle. She was a friend and disciple of Emerson and felt, as indeed every transcendentalist felt, that she had a metaphysical creed to expound. If the writings of this school have left little that is powerful except the Essays of the master himself, nevertheless the spirit of the Oversoul became expressed in the lives of many of his contemporaries. I have known people who wrote philosophy very ill, who yet seemed to have received a kind of heavenly message from stepping in and out of Emerson's library. This species of Emersonianism clung to Mrs. Howe.

Some serene element of the successful person, who lives above circumstance, shone out of her conversation,—which was, by the way, extremely unlike the Concord school of talk. She was always a doughty, gallant battler in the drawing-room, with the old style of attack. She feutered her lance, as was the custom of the forties, and rode her charger straight at the opponent.

The accidents of the world, which had swept away wealth and had left her only a modest little house, and a scanty income, had taken nothing from her. She had always lived in mansions of her own. Her guests were kings and queens to her. If the door had been opened by a charity girl with a wooden leg, and the meal had consisted of a chop on a trencher, the guest would still have felt that he was being welcomed with reverence and was feasting with Hafiz and Melchior. There are people in whom spiritual experiences dissolve self-consciousness, so that all humanity walks for them on the same social plane. Such was the ideal of the antique philosophers, and Mrs. Howe, in a certain way, reminded one of those ancients. Ben Franklin had the same quality in his old age,—a quality which no one ought to attain to in youth; for youth is properly dedicated to error. When Mrs. Howe was young, she was so high-spirited and self-willed that she sometimes became a problem to her friends. Old ladies have told me about her romanticism and her uncontrollability. I knew her only in old age, and when her chief characteristic was an unfailing gayety. It was strange that a woman of causes, whose main business was to worry politicians, arouse the people and do in fact the most unpleasant things a woman can do, never should have betrayed those traces of the work which are seen in almost all public spirited women.

Mrs. Howe was liberal, spontaneous, feminine. Her supreme endowment was her health. She had the domed brow and the bonhomie of a woman who has never been sick. Such people are ever younger than their children; for their children soon grow up into sad, practical men and women, while they themselves retain the buoyancy of youth. The world cannot teach them sorrow. Mrs. Howe thus became the pet of her numerous children, at the same time that she was the Mother Superior of the latest generation of nonconformist philanthropy in Boston. She accepted both posts with enthusiasm.

Her power of enjoyment was a natural advantage, like a large fortune or a great talent, and it was really this force that made her beloved. If she had a weakness, it was the weakness of almost all leaders, the habit of accepting adulation from insignificant people, whom she suffered to rest in the belief that she was a prophetess. But she did this so innocently, and humbly, that I cannot feel sure that her own hopes and illusions as to her greatness were not a part of her charm.

The marvel of her was that she should never have been influenced by Boston. She was not even irritated by the self-sufficiency of Bostonians, by that slight mental cramp in them which is a grief to many of their sincerest admirers. Of course everybody in Boston knew her. One couldn't help knowing her. The policemen knew her; the school-children sang her "Battle Hymn of the Republic"; the statesmen, scholars, scientists, and publicists for a generation regarded her as one of their cherished institutions and as a pillar of the crumbling world. Individual Beacon Street knew her, but not collective Beacon Street. To collective Beacon Street she was *persona non grata.* I remember being a little shocked at the way certain very nice people used to speak of her; though in retrospect, the prejudice which good society has against non-conforming greatness, appears in the light of agreeable local color.

I have often lain awake at night wondering what was the matter with Boston. At such times, anecdotes creep out of corners in my memory and throw doubtful gleams of light on possible solutions. But I cannot catch and chain these ideas. One of my classmates, a modest youth from South Carolina, when he was a Freshman at Harvard, walked into the bosom of a great Boston drawing-room with his overshoes on. All the family were seated about,—the aged and distinguished grandparents, the model father, the benignant mother, and many appropriate children of all ages. My friend was unconscious of his predicament, young and modest. Summoning all of his imperfect Southern breeding, he did his best with the hard beginnings of cheerful talk. But he felt an oppression in the air, then a wave of sympathy,—a sense of humiliation,—a waiting fear. He saw that the younger members of the family were in hurried consultation about something, which he prophetically knew concerned himself. The suspense became unbearable, and at last an appropriate child of the family group drew him aside and whispered to him the awful truth.

My friend told me the story the next day, and I knew instantly, and I know now, that the solution of Boston lay beneath my hand if I had but the wit to see it. But what is it?

Clarence King told me that he happened to be in Boston in 1870, when Bret Harte first appeared upon the extreme Western horizon, with his "Luck of Roaring Camp," and the rest of his wonderful earliest work in his hand. King at once became an object of interest in Boston because he knew Bret Harte, and was taken to lunch with the famous Saturday Club at the Parker House, where Longfellow, Holmes, Emerson, Lowell and the other immortals resorted for pie and for celestial converse. Mr. Longfellow, who was the most gracious gentleman that ever lived, turned to King and asked in regard to Bret Harte—"But is he a genius?" Longfellow pronounced the word "ge-ni-us," and quietly paused for a reply. King said, "Why as to that, Mr. Longfellow, everybody knows that the country possesses no *three-syllabled genius* outside of Massachusetts." "Did they laugh?" I asked of King. "Not a smile," he said. "But afterwards, Dr. Holmes came round during the coffee and cigars and pressed my hand quietly and told me that that was a good thing I had said to Longfellow."

In this anecdote, we get very near the secret. Why didn't those gentlemen laugh? They were the wittiest set in America, fond of laughing, collected at lunch for the very purpose of joking. Yes, but not at *themselves*; and not in response to the jest of a new, raw outsider. Had Dr. Holmes himself made the quip, it would have been repeated all over Boston. But they were not prepared to laugh before knowing whether Clarence King was a wit. Where was his certificate? And who let him in, anyway?

The great, terrible, important powers of the world, like social caste and religious domination, always rest on secrets. A man is born on the wrong side of the street and can therefore never enter into certain drawing-rooms, even though he be in every way superior to everyone in those drawing-rooms. When you try to find out what the difference is between him and the rest, and why he is accursed, you find that the reason is a secret. It is a secret that a certain kind of straw hat is damnable. Little boys know these things about other little boys. The world is written over with mysterious tramp-languages and symbols of Masonic hieroglyphics. I know these things because I belong to the Masonic Lodge of Massachusetts. By the accident of birth I am inside Boston (Aeschylus says that relationship is a tremendous force). I am inside of Boston, and I am going to divulge the meaning of every Masonic symbol which I can decipher.

Boston has always been a hieratic aristocracy. Its chief rulers were parsons in the eighteenth century, and business men in the nineteenth. But you may take it for granted that there was always a pharisaical clique in the middle of Boston, a clique of elders. The anthropologists have no doubt a name for the gang-instinct and cryptic passion that binds thieves together, and fills the words "he is one of us" with so much religious power. Now, amid all the downfall of Puritanism, and of the old Boston cultivation, the inner core of a loyalty to a local priesthood still rules the city; and, on the whole, rules it well. Social Boston is a religious society, so also is business Boston, so is sporting Boston, so is literary Boston. If you know the town well, you will often find persons there who are not of the caste. Their countenances do not fall at the mention of Moses and Aaron, and they wear no phylacteries. You will generally find that such people are mere sojourners in Boston; their fathers and grandfathers came from elsewhere.

One should immerse one's self occasionally in some hieratic influence in order to understand how vulgar and disgusting any merely personal virtue appears in the eyes of the faithful. The devout Protestant is, to the devout Catholic, a gross and boorish person.

The nature of Mrs. Howe's social talents was not acceptable to the taste of Boston. Her house was full of Persians, Armenians, and the professors of strange new faiths. I think it was her followers rather than herself that displeased the Bostonians. She sat at the gate and entertained all men, including a lot of people who Boston thought ought not to be entertained. But there she sat, nevertheless,—all courage, all wit and all benignity, and so will the image of her ever remain in the minds of the thousands of those who knew her.

[1915]

Maria Weston Chapman

Maria Weston Chapman deserves a medallion in the historic hall of her generation. Indeed she looked and bore herself like bronze and marble, and made upon all observers the impression of heroic womanhood. There are women who have a maturity in their walk even in their teens, and who carry a girlish bearing into old age. There is a unity and a focus in their being which makes them distinguished. In all they do or say there is some natural force which is inevitable and spontaneous. All this is largely a matter of physical endowment, and goes with abundant health. In my grandmother's case it went with a kind of victorious beauty which became accentuated as the "cordage of the countenance" declared itself in her latest years.

As a small child I was immensely impressed with her. I had never seen anyone like her. She looked like a cameo, and yet had a buoyant—I had almost said bounding—quality which cameos do not suggest. Many persons in her generation were imposing, but she was the first of them that I ever saw, and this gave me a new idea of how people of the great world might or ought to appear. She had a talent for conduct, she had a genius for appearance. She was exactly fitted to lead a cause; and the cause of Abolition, which broke into flame during her girlhood, was a most perfect and typical example of what a cause can be. It was a religious awakening. It began with great and sudden fervor in the breasts of a few people, and worked in such a manner as to separate these people from the rest of the community. To awaken the rest of America became their one idea. Converts came to them, as is usual in such cases, chiefly from the humbler classes; and the emotional fervor of the movement burned with a steady heat for thirty years, till in one way or another every individual in the nation was reached by it. The Abolitionists are sometimes blamed for causing the war; but the real cause of the war was human nature. The war was the final working out of a great change. Abolition was merely the symptom that a change had begun.

Mrs. Chapman was an early convert, and was well fitted to take the lead in such a movement, or, more accurately speaking, to stage and conduct the cause; for Garrison was her leader, and she was in every sense a standard-bearer and a lieutenant,—never, properly speaking, the leader. She was always handsomely dressed, smiling, dominant, ready to meet all comers. She entered a room like a public person. She was a doughty swordswoman in conversation, and wore armor. There was something about her that reminded me of a gladiator, and I sometimes wondered how she had ever borne children at all and whether she had nursed them, or had just marched off to the wars in Gaul and Iberia, while the urchins were being cared for by a freed-woman in the Campania. She was fond of children nevertheless, and used to invite her grandchildren to come to her room, where she would inaugurate the most ceremonious and important sessions of book-covering, and the making of scrapbooks, cuttings, and pastings. The gum-arabic must be bought and melted down on the previous day, the figured papers and prints were produced from European sources, and the whole manufacture was conducted with pomp and mystery. She used to read Shakespeare to us when the youngest was about three, and she would arrange the drawing-room to represent the stage.

She had Caesar on his bier covered with drapery, and a bit of hidden marble to represent his Roman nose. When she read aloud she was so particular about the state of her voice, her enunciation, and her delivery that she would eat no dinner before a performance, but take only the juice of a lemon—as if she were to sing in grand opera.

I think that her temperament and physique must in early life have marked her as a figure-head, and that the many years she afterwards spent in Europe as the representative of a cause gave her, perhaps, the habit of the part. She was, in fact, an *embodiment*; and this is the reason why her presence conveyed more than her spoken or written words, and why people were so astonished at her, and have left so many descriptions of her. At the basis of her effectiveness was a perfectly phenomenal fund of physical health. She was beaming and ruddy down to her last days—for she was nearly eighty when she died, and had spent many years toward the end of her life in nursing a paralyzed brother.

One great and rare merit she shared with Garrison. When their cause triumphed they retired, and both of them deserve in this to be canonized for their good taste,—a virtue not always found in Abolitionists. She retired, then, and lived in Weymouth, Massachusetts, for twenty years or more, with a mother and several sisters, all of them highly educated, bookish people, and two of them, Anne and Dora Weston, staunch anti-slavery veterans. The house was full of souvenirs of Europe, and of presentation copies of the works of mid-century European writers. To be an exile for opinion's sake is the best introduction to the liberals of all foreign countries; and Paris, during the Second Empire, contained many distinguished Frenchmen who felt that they too were in exile. The French intellectuals were hospitable to the leaders of American anti-slavery, who, so far as social life went, found in France more than they had lost at home.

All the glamour and excitement of life must have gone out of it for my grandmother with the close of the war; yet she continued to live as freshly and to talk as gladly as if some persecution were still in progress, and she were Joan of Arc on the way to the pyre.

Certain failings she had,—perhaps I ought rather to call them never-failings. The sword would leap from the scabbard at any allusion to past controversy in which she or Mr. Garrison had been concerned, or in which anyone in the world had held opinions condemned by the Garrisonians. The sword of Gideon flashed with unabated grace. The indignation was as fresh as manna in Arabia—renewed with every matin. She really believed that the memory of the wicked should rot, and that the wicked were—almost everyone in the past, and a good many among the survivors. If Channing had been wrong in 1828, she would excoriate him in 1882. If Sumner had hesitated at some moment to see the white light of truth, then his bones must be dragged from their resting place and his habitation become a dunghill. Among the true, inner-seal Garrisonians the *wrong kind* of anti-slavery was always considered as anti-Christ; and the feats of memory which the Old Guard of Abolition exhibited with regard to the ins and outs of ancient controversy went far to explain the survival of Homer's poems throughout the long centuries before writing was invented. So, as by fire, are certain things burned into men's souls.

I must here sorrowfully record a distinction between my grandmother and Garrison himself. Garrison was never rancorous, at least he was never really rancorous. His rancor was political and done for effect. He assumed a tone of malevolence for rhetorical reasons. Now, my grandmother became, by a kind of necessity, more religious than the Pope himself. She was a partisan: she had not the liberty which the leader enjoys of changing her mind, or of being inconsistently good-humored when she felt like it. She was a halberdier and body-guard. She never seemed to disagree with Mr. Garrison or to turn a critical eye on him. I believe it would have done them both good if she had lifted her battle-ax against the hero now and then.

For twenty-five years she was manager of the Annual Antislavery Bazaar which raised the funds for the cause. Europe was laid under contribution for interesting and odd things, which should draw Pro-Slavery Boston to the booths. The preparation for the great Fair went on pretty steadily during the rest of the year, and this branch of anti-slavery propaganda was useful in keeping the liberals in Europe in touch with our struggle. Mrs. Chapman edited a little annual volume or keepsake, called "The Liberty Bell," which contained many articles by herself. As the executive of an unpopular cause her business was to be always in good spirits, always in the right, always insuperably competent. It is clear that her activity belongs to a very noble species of political activity rather than to the field of philosophy. The religion of labor makes character, but is injurious to mind. And I cannot help thinking of all the anti-slavery people as being earth-born, titanic creatures, whom Nature spawned to stay a plague—and then withdrew them, and broke the mold. Heroic they remain.

It will be remembered that our struggle over slavery showed up the organized churches of Christianity in a terrible light. What was the use of such churches as ours were shown to be? Where was Christ to be found in them? If an Abolitionist were by nature a mystic, or an evangelical person (like Garrison or S.J. May), he naturally took refuge in the New Testament itself. If he were by nature neither mystical nor romantic, he was apt to become a stoic; and it was to this class that my grandmother belonged. We may see the same tendency exhibited on a great scale in the history of France. The hold which the classics have on the French temperament is due to this,—that the French are not sufficiently emotional to be in sympathy with Hebrew thought: it offends them. The morality of France is stoical. My grandmother was, in her endowments, and in her limitations, very much such a person as a virtuous stoic of the ancient world may have been. Her religion was a totality as to conduct, but was fragmentary in statement. It was made up of proverbs, poems, and anecdotes from all ages,—wisdom-scraps of an encouraging and militant nature. When the original Garrisonians began their work in 1832 they supposed that slavery would fall before their strokes in a very few years,—five or ten perhaps. And so subtly does the alchemy of activity sustain hope, that they never for a moment lost their conviction that victory was imminent, throughout the thirty years during which victory kept receding before them like the mirage of water in the desert. They only wondered at the delay.

A Cause like this solves all questions whether they be matters of metaphysical doubt or of practical life. One's business is ruined, of course. A child dies; alas, it is severe, but let the Cause consume our grief. All social ties were snapped long ago; it is a trifle. The old standard-bearers are dropping out from time to time through death; peace be unto them, we have others.

The discipline of such a life—so unusual, so singular—wore down men and women into athletes; the stress made them strong. Thus the anti-slavery fighters grew hardy through a sort of Roman endurance, which shows in their physiognomy. It is this force behind the stroke of fate that we see in people's faces,— the power behind the die that mints them.

A very notable feature in my grandmother's life was her friendship with Harriet Martineau, whose literary executor she afterwards became. The friendship was a flawless and enduring union. It began in 1835, and was a source of unalloyed happiness to both women; it ended with Miss Martineau's death in 1876. The attachment was accompanied by independence on both sides, but my grandmother used to speak of Harriet Martineau with the same sort of reverence that Miss Martineau uses in speaking of her.

At one time Miss Martineau thought of coming to America to work in the Abolition cause. She writes: "The discovery of her [Mrs. Chapman's] moral power and insight were to me so extraordinary that, while I longed to work with and under her, I felt that it must be morally perilous to lean on any one mind as I could not but lean on hers."

The beginning of their intimacy was not without dramatic interest. When Miss Martineau arrived in this country on a pleasure trip, at the age of thirty-three, she was probably the best known, and certainly the most powerful woman in England. Her writings and her opinions had brought her unprecedented popularity both in that country and in America. It was therefore of great importance to the struggling Abolitionists to gain her adherence to their cause. My grandmother wrote to Miss Martineau while the latter was on her travels in the South, but received a rebuff from the authoress.

The time soon came, however, when Miss Martineau felt forced by her conscience to support the unpopular and hated cause of Abolition. She was, as she says, unexpectedly and very reluctantly, but necessarily, implicated in the struggle. The occasion of her declaration of faith was a meeting of the Ladies' Anti-slavery Society at the house of Francis Jackson on November 18, 1835. She accepted an invitation to this meeting and, when called upon, gave, in a few words, the enormous prestige of her name to the cause. This cut short her social career in America, and she became the victim of every kind of vilification. She understood this consequence and did not enjoy it, for it ruined her trip and prevented her seeing American social life.

But the greater moral triumph at the back of this small unpleasantness was also understood both by Miss Martineau and by the audience of women in the hushed parlor of Francis Jackson, at the time she expressed her anti-slavery conviction in a few solemn words. It must be noted parenthetically that everyone who speaks of my grandmother always dwells upon the way she looked. It is her looks that they cannot forget.

Miss Martineau in her account of the meeting at Mr. Jackson's says: "When I was putting on my shawl upstairs, Mrs. Chapman came to me, bonnet in hand, to say, 'You know we are threatened with a mob again to-day: but I do not myself much apprehend it. It must not surprise us; but my hopes are stronger than my fears.'

"I hear now, as I write, the clear silvery tones of her who was to be the friend of the rest of my life. I still see the exquisite beauty which took me by surprise that day; the slender, graceful form, the golden hair which might have covered her feet; the brilliant complexion, noble profile, and deep blue eyes; the aspect meant by nature to be soft and winning only, but that day (as ever since), so vivified by courage, and so strengthened by upright conviction, as to appear the very embodiment of heroism. 'My hopes,' she said as she threw up her golden hair under her bonnet, 'are stronger than my fears.'"

In the same account Miss Martineau describes the extreme tension that existed concerning her own attitude toward Abolition. No one knew just where she stood, or what she was going to say. She describes also the wave of emotion that swept over the little assemblage upon her unequivocal announcement of her hatred of slavery, and continues: "As I concluded Mrs. Chapman bowed down her glowing face on her folded arms, and there was a murmur of satisfaction through the room, while outside, the growing crowd (which did not, however, become large) was hooting and yelling and throwing mud and dirt against the windows."

[1914]

Learning

An expert on Greek Art chanced to describe in my hearing one of the engraved gems in the Metropolitan Museum. He spoke of it as "certainly one of the great gems of the world," and there was something in his tone that was even more thrilling than his words. He might have been describing the Parthenon or Beethoven's Mass,—such was the passion of reverence that flowed out of him as he spoke. I went to see the gem afterwards. It was badly placed, and for all artistic purposes was invisible. I suppose that even if I had had a good look at it, I should not have been able to appreciate its full merit. Who could?—save the handful of adepts in the world, the little group of gem-readers, by whom the mighty music of this tiny score could be read at first sight.

Nevertheless it was a satisfaction to me to have seen the stone. I knew that through its surface there poured the power of the Greek world; that not without Phidias and Aristotle, and not without the Parthenon, could it have come into existence. It carried in its bosom a digest of the visual laws of spiritual force, and was as wonderful and as sacred as any stone could well be.

Its value to mankind was not to be measured by my comprehension of it, but was inestimable. As Petrarch felt toward the Greek manuscript of Homer which he owned but could not read, so did I feel toward the gem.

What is Education? What are Art and Religion and all those higher interests in civilization which are always vaguely held up to us as being the most important things in life? These things elude definition. They cannot be put into words except through the interposition of what the Germans call "a metaphysic." Before you can introduce them into discourse, you must step aside for a moment and create a theory of the universe; and by the time you have done this, you have perhaps befogged and exhausted your readers. Let us be content with a more modest ambition. It is possible to take a general view of the externals of these subjects without losing reverence for their realities. It is possible to consider the forms under which art and religion appear,—the algebra and notation by which they have expressed themselves in the past,—and to draw some general conclusion as to the nature of the subject, without becoming entangled in the subject itself.

We may deal with the influence of the gem without striving exactly to translate its meaning into speech. We all concede its importance. We know, for instance, that the admiration of my friend the expert was no accident. He found in the design and workmanship of the intaglio the same ideas which he had been at work on all his life. Greek culture long ago had become a part of this man's brain, and its hieroglyphs expressed what to him was religion. So of all monuments, languages, and arts which descend to us out of the past. The peoples are dead, but the documents remain; and these documents themselves are part of a living and intimate tradition which also descends to us out of the past,—a tradition so familiar and native to the brain that we forget its origin. We almost believe that our feeling for art is original with us. We are tempted to think there is some personal and logical reason at the back of all grammar, whether it be the grammar of speech or the grammar of architecture,—so strong is the appeal to our taste made by traditional usage. Yet the great reason of the power of art is the historic reason. "In this manner have these things been expressed: in similar manner must they continue to be said." So speaks our artistic instinct.

Good usage has its sanction, like religion or government. We transmit the usage without pausing to think why we do so. We instinctively correct a child, without pausing to reflect that the fathers of the race are speaking through us. When the child says, "Give me a apple," we correct him—"You must say, 'An apple.'" What the child really means, in fact, is an apple.

All teaching is merely a way of acquainting the learner with the body of existing tradition. If the child is ever to have anything to say of his own, he has need of every bit of this expressive medium to help him do it. The reason is, that, so far as expressiveness goes, only one language exists. Every experiment and usage of the past is a part of this language. A phrase or an idea rises in the Hebrew, and filters through the Greek or Latin and French down to our own time. The practitioners who scribble and dream in words from their childhood up,—into whose habit of thought language is kneaded through a thousand reveries,—these are the men who receive, reshape, and transmit it. Language is their portion, they are the priests of language.

The same thing holds true of the other vehicles of idea, of painting, architecture, religion, etc., but since we have been speaking of language, let us continue to speak of language. Expressiveness follows literacy. The poets have been tremendous readers always. Petrarch, Dante, Chaucer, Shakespeare, Milton, Goethe, Byron, Keats—those of them who possessed not much of the foreign languages had a passion for translations. It is amazing how little of a foreign language you need if you have a passion for the thing written in it. We think of Shakespeare as of a lightly-lettered person; but he was ransacking books all day to find plots and language for his plays. He reeks with mythology, he swims in classical metaphor: and, if he knew the Latin poets only in translation, he knew them with that famished intensity of interest which can draw the meaning through the walls of a bad text. Deprive Shakespeare of his sources, and he could not have been Shakespeare.

Good poetry is the echoing of shadowy tongues, the recovery of forgotten talent, the garment put up with perfumes. There is a passage in the *Tempest* which illustrates the free-masonry of artistic craft, and how the weak sometimes hand the torch to the mighty. Prospero's apostrophe to the spirits is, surely, as Shakespearian as anything in Shakespeare and as beautiful as anything in imaginative poetry.

> "Ye elves of hills, brooks, standing lakes and groves;
> And ye, that in the sands with printless foot
> Do chase the ebbing Neptune, and do fly him,
> When he comes back; you demi-puppets, that
> By moonshine do the sour ringlets make,
> Whereof the ewe not bites; and you whose pastime
> Is to make midnight mushrooms that rejoice
> To hear the solemn curfew; by whose aid
> (Weak masters though ye be) I have bedimmed
> The noontide sun, called forth the mutinous winds,
> And 'twixt the green sea and the azur'd vault
> Set roaring war: to the dread rattling thunder
> Have I given fire, and rifted Jove's stout oak
> With his own bolt: the strong-bas'd promontory
> Have I made shake; and by the spurs pluck'd up
> The pine and cedar: graves at my command
> Have waked their sleepers; oped and let them forth
> By my so potent art."

Shakespeare borrowed this speech from Medea's speech in Ovid, which he knew in the translation of Arthur Golding; and really Shakespeare seems almost to have held the book in his hand while penning Prospero's speech. The following is from Golding's translation, published in 1567:

"Ye Ayres and windes; ye Elves of Hilles and Brooks, of
    Woods alone,
Of standing Lakes and of the Night approach ye every
    chone.
Through helpe of whom (the crooked banks much
    wondering at the thing)
I have compelled streams to run clean backward to their
    spring.
By charmes I make the calm seas rough, and make the
    rough Seas plaine.
And cover all the Skie with Clouds and chase them thence
    again.
By charmes I raise and lay the windes, and burst the Viper's
    jaw.
And from the bowels of the Earth both stones and trees doe
    draw.
Whole woods and Forestes I remove: I make the Mountains
    shake,
And even the Earth it selfe to grone and fearfully to quake.
I call up dead men from their graves: and thee O lightsome
    Moone
I darken oft, though beaten brasse abate thy perill soone.
Our Sorcerie dims the Morning faire, and darkes the Sun at
    Noone.
The flaming breath of fierie Bulles ye quenched for my
    sake.
And caused their unwieldie neck the bended yokes to take.
Among the Earthbred brothers you a mortell war did set
And brought a sleepe the Dragon fell whose eyes were never
    shut."

There is, and is to be, no end of this reappearance of old metaphor, old trade secret, old usage of art. No sooner has a masterpiece appeared, that summarizes all knowledge, than men get up eagerly the next morning with chisel and brush, and try again. Nothing done satisfies. It is all in the making that the inspiration lies; and this endeavor renews itself with the ages, and grows by devouring its own offspring.

The technique of any art is the whole body of experimental knowledge through which the art speaks. The glazes of pottery become forgotten and have to be hit upon over again. The knack of Venetian glass, the principle of effect in tiles, in lettering, in the sonnet, in the fugue, in the tower,—all the prestidigitation of art that is too subtle to be named or thought of, must yet be acquired and kept up by practice, held to by constant experiment.

Good artistic expression is thus not only a thing done: it is a way of life, a habit of breathing, a mode of unconsciousness, a world of being which records itself as it unrolls. We call this world Art for want of a better name; but the thing that we value is the life within, not the shell of the creature. This shell is what is left behind in the passage of time, to puzzle our after-study and make us wonder how it was made, how such complex delicacy and power ever came to co-exist. I have often wondered over the *Merchant of Venice* as one wonders over a full-blown transparent poppy that sheds light and blushes like a cloud. Neither the poppy nor the play were exactly hewn out: they grew, they expanded and bloomed by a sort of inward power,— unconscious, transcendent. The fine arts blossom from the old stock,—from the poppy-seed of the world.

I am here thinking of the whole body of the arts, the vehicles through which the spirit of man has been expressed. I am thinking also of the sciences,—whose refractory, belligerent worshipers are even less satisfied with any past expression than the artists are, for their mission is to destroy and to rearrange. They would leave nothing alive but themselves. Nevertheless, science has always been obliged to make use of written language in recording her ideas. The sciences are as much a part of recorded language as are the arts. No matter how revolutionary scientific thought may be, it must resort to metaphysics when it begins to formulate its ultimate meanings. Now when you approach metaphysics, the Greek and the Hebrew have been there before you: you are very near to matters which perhaps you never intended to approach. You are back at the beginning of all things. In fact, human thought does not advance, it only recurs. Every tone and semi-tone in the scale is a keynote; and every point in the Universe is the centre of the Universe; and every man is the centre and focus of the cosmos, and through him passes the whole of all force, as it exists and has existed from eternity; hence the significance which may at any moment radiate out of anything.

The different arts and devices that time hands to us are like our organs. They are the veins and arteries of humanity. You cannot rearrange them or begin anew. Your verse-forms and your architecture are chosen for you, like your complexion and your temperament. The thing you desire to express is in them already. Your labors do no more than enable you to find your own soul in them. If you will begin any piece of artistic work in an empirical spirit and slave over it until it suits you, you will find yourself obliged to solve all the problems which the artists have been engaged on since the dawn of history. Be as independent as you like, you will find that you have been anticipated at every point: you are a slave to precedent, because precedent has done what you are trying to do, and, ah, how much better! In the first place, the limitations, the horrible limitations of artistic possibility, will begin to present themselves; few things can be done: they have all been tried: they have all been worked to death: they have all been developed by immortal genius and thereafter avoided by lesser minds,—left to await more immortal genius. The field of endeavor narrows itself in proportion to the greatness of the intellect that is at work. In ages of great art everyone knows what the problem is and how much is at stake. Masaccio died at the age of twenty-seven, after having painted half a dozen pictures which influenced all subsequent art, because they showed to Raphael the best solution of certain technical questions. The Greeks of the best period were so very knowing that everything appeared to them ugly except the few attitudes, the few arrangements, which were capable of being carried to perfection.

Anyone who has something to say is thus found to be in one sense a slave, but a rich slave who has inherited the whole earth. If you can only obey the laws of your slavery, you become an emperor: you are only a slave in so far as you do not understand how to use your wealth. If you have but the gift of submission, you conquer. Many tongues, many hands, many minds, a traditional state of feeling, traditional symbols,—the whole passed through the eyes and soul of a single man,—such is art, such is human expression in all its million-sided variety.

II.

I have thrown together these remarks in an elliptical and haphazard way, hoping to show what sort of thing education is, and as a prologue to a few reflections upon the educational conditions in the United States.

It is easy to think of reasons why the standards of general education should be low in America. Almost every influence which is hostile to the development of deep thought and clear feeling has been at the maximum of destructive power in the United States. We are a new society, made of a Babel of conflicting European elements, engaged in exploiting the wealth of a new continent, under conditions of climate which involve a nervous reorganization to Europeans who come to live with us. Our history has been a history of quiet colonial beginnings, followed by a national life which, from its inception, has been one of social unrest. And all this has happened during the great epoch of the expansion of commerce, the thought-destroying epoch of the world.

Let us take a rapid glance at our own past. In the beginning we were settlers. Now the settlement of any new continent plays havoc with the arts and crafts. Let us imagine that among the Mayflower pilgrims there had been a few expert wood-carvers, a violin player or two, and a master architect. These men, upon landing in the colony, must have been at a loss for employment. They would have to turn into backwoodsmen. Their accomplishments would in time have been forgotten. Within a generation after the landing of the pilgrims there must have followed a decline in the fine arts, in scholarship, and in certain kinds of social refinement. This decline was, to some extent, counteracted in our colonial era by the existence of wealth in the Colonies and by the constant intercourse with Europe, from which the newest models were imported by every vessel. Nevertheless, it is hard for a colony to make up for its initial loss; and we have recently seen the United States government making efforts on a large scale to give to the American farmer those practices of intensive cultivation of the soil which he lost by becoming a backwoodsman and has never since had time to recover for himself.

The American Revolution was our second serious set-back in education. So hostile to culture is war that the artisans of France have never been able to attain to the standards of workmanship which prevailed under the old monarchy. Our national culture started with the handicap of a seven years' war, and was always a little behindhand. During the nineteenth century the American citizen has been buffeting the waves of new development. His daily life has been an experiment. His moral, social, political interests and duties have been indeterminate; nothing has been settled for him by society. Is a man to have an opinion? Then he must make it himself. This demands a more serious labor than if he were obliged to manufacture his own shoes and candlesticks. No such draught upon individual intellect is made in an old country. You cannot get a European to understand this distressing over-taxing of the intelligence in America. Nothing like it has occurred before, because in old countries opinion is part of caste and condition: opinion is the shadow of interest and of social status.

But in America the individual is not protected against society at large by the bulwark of his class. He stands by himself. It is a noble idea that a man should stand by himself, and the conditions which force a man to do so have occasionally created magnificent types of heroic manhood in America. Lincoln, Garrison, Emerson, and many lesser athletes are the fruits of these very conditions which isolate the individual in America and force him to think for himself. Yet their effect upon general cultivation has been injurious. It seems as if character were always within the reach of every human soul; but men must have become homogeneous before they can produce art.

We have thus reviewed a few of the causes of our American loss of culture. Behind all these causes, however, was the true and overmastering cause, namely, that sudden creation of wealth for which the nineteenth century is noted, the rise all over the world of new and uneducated classes. We came into being as a part of that world movement which has perceptibly retarded culture, even in Europe. How, then, could we in America hope to resist it? Whether this movement is the result of democratic ideas, or of mechanical inventions, or of scientific discovery, no one can say. The elements that go to make up the movement cannot be unraveled. We only know that the world has changed: the old order has vanished with all its charm, with all its experience, with all its refinement. In its place we have a crude world, indifferent to everything except physical well-being. In the place of the fine arts and the crafts we have business and science.

Business is, of course, devoted to the increase of physical well-being; but what is Science? Now, in one sense, science is anything that the scientific men of the moment happen to be studying. In one decade, science means the discussion of spontaneous generation, or spontaneous variation, in the next of plasm, in the next of germs, or of electrodes. Whatever the scientific world takes up as a study becomes "science." It is impossible to deny the truth of this rather self-destructive definition. In a more serious sense, however, science is the whole body of organized knowledge; and a distinction is sometimes made between "pure" science and "applied" science; the first being concerned solely with the ascertainment of truth, the second, with practical matters.

In these higher regions, in which science is synonymous with the search for truth, science partakes of the nature of religion. It purifies its votaries; it speaks to them in cryptic language, revealing certain exalted realities not unrelated to the realities of music, or of poetry and religion. The men through whom this enthusiasm for pure science passes are surely, each in his degree, transmitters of heroic influence; and, in their own way, they form a kind of priesthood. It must be confessed, too, that this priesthood is peculiarly the product of the nineteenth century.

The Brotherhood of Science is a new order, a new Dispensation. It would seem to me impossible to divide one's feeling toward science according to the divisions "pure" and "applied"; because many men in whom the tide of true enthusiasm runs the strongest deal in applied science, as, for instance, surgeons, bacteriologists, etc. Nor ought we to forget those great men of science who have an attitude of sympathy toward all human excellence, and a reverence for things which cannot be approached through science. Such men resemble those saints who have also, incidentally, been kings and popes. Their personal magnitude obliterates our interest in their position in the hierarchy. We think of them as men, not as popes, kings or scientists. In the end we must admit that there are as many kinds of science as there are of men engaged in scientific pursuits. The word science legitimately means an immense variety of things, loosely connected together, some of them deserving of strong reprobation. I shall use the term with such accuracy as I am able to command, and leave it to the candid reader to make allowance for whatever injustice this course may entail.

To begin with, we must find fault with the Brotherhood of Science on much the same ground that we fought the old religions, upon grounds of tyranny and narrowness, of dogmatism and presumption. In the next place, it is evident that, in so far as science is not hallowed by the spirit of religion, it is a mere extension of business. It is the essence of world-business, race-business, cosmic-business. It saves time, saves lives, and dominates the air and the sea; but all these things may be accomplished, for ought we know, in the course of the extinction of the better nature of mankind. Science is not directly interested in the expression of spiritual truth; her notation cannot include anything so fluctuating, so indeterminate, as the language of feeling. Science neither sings nor jokes; neither prays nor rejoices; neither loves nor hates. This is not her fault; but her limitation. Her fault is that, as a rule, she respects only her own language and puts trust only in what is in her own shop window.

I deprecate the contempt which science expresses for anything that does not happen to be called science. Imperial and haughty science proclaims its occupancy of the whole province of human thought; yet, as a matter of fact, science deals in a language of its own, in a set of formulae and conceptions which cannot cover the most important interests of humanity. It does not understand the value of the fine arts and is always at loggerheads with philosophy. Is it not clear that science, in order to make good her claim to universality, must adopt a conception of her own function that shall leave to the fine arts and to religion their languages? She cannot hope to compete with these languages, nor to translate or expound them. She must accept them. At present she tramples upon them.

There are, then, in the modern world these two influences which are hostile to education,—the influence of business and the influence of uninspired science. In Europe these influences are qualified by the vigor of the old learning. In America they dominate remorselessly, and make the path of education doubly hard. Consider how they meet us in ordinary social life. We have all heard men bemoan the time they have spent over Latin and Greek on the ground that these studies did not fit them for business,—as if a thing must be worthless if it can be neither eaten nor drunk. It is hard to explain the value of education to men who have forgotten the meaning of education: its symbols convey nothing to them.

The situation is very similar in dealing with scientific men,— at least with that large class of them who have little learning and no religion, and who are thus obliged to use the formulae of modern science as their only vehicle of thought. These men regard humanity as something which started up in Darwin's time. They do not listen when the humanities are mentioned;

and if they did they would not understand. When Darwin confessed that poetry had no meaning for him, and that nothing significant was left to him in the whole artistic life of the past, he did not know how many of his brethren his words were destined to describe.

We can forgive the business man for the loss of his birthright: he knows no better. But we have it against a scientist if he undervalues education. Surely, the Latin classics are as valuable a deposit as the crustacean fossils, or the implements of the Stone Age. When science shall have assumed her true relation to the field of human culture we shall all be happier. To-day science knows that the silkworm must be fed on the leaves of the mulberry tree, but does not know that the soul of man must be fed on the Bible and the Greek classics. Science knows that a queen bee can be produced by care and feeding, but does not as yet know that every man who has had a little Greek and Latin in his youth belongs to a different species from the ignorant man. No matter how little it may have been, it reclassifies him. There is more kinship between that man and a great scholar than there is between the same man and some one who has had no classics at all: he breathes from a different part of his anatomy. Drop the classics from education? Ask rather, Why not drop education? For the classics are education. We cannot draw a line and say, "Here we start." The facts are the other way. We started long ago, and our very life depends upon keeping alive all that we have thought and felt during our history. If the continuity is taken from us, we shall relapse.

When we discover that these two tremendous interests—business and commercial science have arisen in the modern world and are muffling the voice of man, we tremble for the future. If these giants shall continue their subjugation of the gods, the whole race, we fear, may relapse into dumbness. By good fortune, however, there are other powers at work. The race is emotionally too rich and too much attached to the past to allow its faculties to be lost through disuse. New and spontaneous crops will soon be growing upon the mould of our own stubbly, thistle-bearing epoch.

In the meantime we in America must do the best we can. It is no secret that our standards of education are below those of Europe. Our art, our historical knowledge, our music and general conversation, show a stiffness and lack of exuberance—a lack of vitality and of unconscious force—the faults of beginners in all walks of life. During the last twenty-five years much improvement has been made in those branches of cultivation which depend directly upon wealth. Since the Civil War there seems to have been a decline in the higher literature, accompanied by an advance in the plastic arts. And more recently still there has been a literary reawakening, perhaps not of the most important kind, yet signifying a new era. If I may employ an obvious simile, I would liken America to a just-grown man of good impulses who has lacked early advantages. He feels that cultivation belongs to him; and yet he cannot catch it nor hold it. He feels the impulse of expression, and yet he can neither read nor write. He feels that he is fitted for general society, and yet he has no current ideas or conversation. And, of course—I say it with regret, but it is a part of the situation—of course he is heady and proud of himself.

What do we all desire for this ingenuous youth on whom the postponed expectation of the world, as Emerson called it, has waited so long? We desire only to furnish him with true advantages. Let us take a simultaneous survey of the two extremities of the youth's education, namely, of nursery training and of the higher education. The two are more intimately dependent upon each other than is generally suspected. With regard to the nursery, early advantages are the key to education. The focus of all cultivation is the fireside. Learning is a stove plant that lives in the cottage and thrives during the long winter in domestic warmth. Unless it be borne into children in their earliest years, there is little hope for it. The whole future of civilization depends upon what is read to children before they can read to themselves. The world is powerless to reconvey itself through any mind that it has not lived in from the beginning,—so hard is the language of symbols, whether in music, or in poetry, or in painting. The art must expand with the heart, as a hot rod of glass is touched by the gold-leaf, and is afterwards blown into dusty stars and rainbows of mantling irradiation. If the glass expands before it has been touched by the metal, there is no means of ever getting the metal into it.

The age of machinery has peopled this continent with promoters and millionaires, and the work of a thousand years has been done in a century. The thing has, however, been accomplished at some cost. An ignorant man makes a fortune and demands the higher education for his children. But it is too late: he should have given it to them when he was in his shirt sleeves. All that they are able to receive now is something very different from education. In receiving it they drag down the old standards. School and college are filled with illiterates. The whole land must patiently wait till Learning has warmed back to life her chilled and starved descendants. Perhaps the child or grandchild of the fortune-builder will teach the children on his knee what he himself learned too late in life to stead him much.

Hunger and thirst for learning is a passion that comes, as it were, out of the ground; now in an age of wealth, now in an age of poverty. Young men are born whom nothing will satisfy except the arts and the sciences. They seek out some scholar at a university and aim at him from boyhood. They persuade their parents to send them to college. They are bored and fatigued by everything that life offers except this thing. Now, society does not create this hunger. All that society can do is to provide nourishment of the right kind, good instruction, true learning, the best scholarship which history has left behind. I believe that to-day there is a spirit of learning abroad in America—here and there, in the young—the old insatiable passion. I feel as if men were arising—most of them still handicapped by the lack of early training—to whom life has no meaning except as a search for truth. This exalted famine of the young scholar is the hope of the world. It is religion and art and science in the chrysalis. The thing which society must beware of doing is of interposing between the young learner and his natural food some mechanical product or patent food of its own. Good culture means the whole of culture in its original sources; bad culture is any substitute for this.

Let us now examine the higher departments of education, the university, the graduate school, the museum,—the learned world in America. There is one function of learned men which is the same in every age, namely, the production of text-books. Learned men shed text-books as the oak sheds acorns, and by their fruits ye shall know them. Open almost any primary text-book or school book in America, and you will, on almost every page of it, find inelegancies of usage, roughnesses, inaccuracies, and occasional errors of grammar. The book has been written by an incompetent hand. Now, what has the writer lacked? Is it grammar? Is it acquaintance with English literature, with good models, with the Bible, with history? It is all these things, and more than all. No school-room teaching can make a man write good English. No school teaching ever made an educated man, or a man who could write a good primary text-book. It requires a home of early culture, supplemented by the whole curriculum of scholarship and of university training. Nothing else but this great engine will produce that little book.

The same conditions prevail in music. If you employ the nearest excellent young lady music teacher to teach your boys to play the piano, she will bring into the house certain child's music written by American composers, in which the rules of harmony are violated and of which the sentiment is vulgar. The books have been written by incompetent people. There is a demand for such books and they are produced. They are the best the times afford: let us be glad that they exist at all and that they are no worse. But note this: it will require the whole musical impulse of the age, from the oratorio society and the musical college down to the street organ, to correct the grammar of that child's music book. Ten or twenty years from now a like book will perhaps be brought into your home, filled with better harmony and with truer musical feeling; and the change will have been wrought through the influence of Sebastian Bach, of Beethoven,—of the masters of music.

It is the same with all things. The higher culture must hang over the cradle, over the professional school, over the community. If you read the lives of the painters of Italy or of the musicians of Germany, you will find that, no matter where a child of genius was born, there was always an educated man to be found in the nearest village—a priest or a schoolmaster—who gave the child the rudiments himself, and became the means of sending him to the university. Without this indigent scholar, where would have been the great master?

It is familiarity with greatness that we need—an early and first-hand acquaintance with the thinkers of the world, whether their mode of thought was music or marble or canvas or language. Their meaning is not easy to come at, but in so far as it reaches us it will transform us. A strange thing has occurred in America. I am not sure that is has ever occurred before. The teachers wish to make learning easy. They desire to prepare and peptonize and sweeten the food. Their little books are soft biscuit for weak teeth, easy reading on great subjects; but these books are filled with a pervading error: they contain a subtle perversion of education.

Learning is not easy, but hard; culture is severe. The steps to Parnassus are steep and terribly arduous. This truth is often forgotten among us; and yet there are fields of work in which it is not forgotten, and in such fields art springs up. Let us remember the accomplishments of our country. The art in which we now most excel is architecture. America has in it many beautiful buildings and some learned architects. And how has this come about? Through severe and conscientious study of the monuments of art, through humble, old-fashioned training. The architects have had first-rate text-books, generally written by Europeans, the non-peptonized, gritty, serious language of masters in the craft. Our painters have done something of the same sort. They have gone to Europe, and are conversant with what is being done in Europe. If they are developing their art here, they do it not ignorantly, but with experience, with consciousness of the past.

I do not recommend subserviency to Europe, but subserviency to intellect. Recourse to Europe we must have: our scholars must absorb Europe without themselves becoming absorbed. It is a curious thing that the American who comes in contact with the old world exhibits two opposite faults: he is often too much impressed and loses stamina, or he is too little impressed and remains a barbarian. Contact with the past and hard work are the cure for both tendencies. Europe is merely an incidental factor in the problem of our education, and this is very well shown in our conduct of our law schools. The Socratic method of instruction in law schools was first introduced at Harvard, and since then it has spread to many parts of the world. This is undoubtedly one of our best achievements in scholarship; and Europe had, so far as I know, no hand in it. The method consists in the *viva voce* discussion of leading cases, text-books being used merely as an auxiliary: the student thus attacks the sources themselves. Here we have American scholarship at its best, and it is precisely the same thing as the European article: it is simply scholarship.

If we can exhibit this spirit in one branch of learning, why not in all? The Promethean fire is one single element. A spark of this fire is all that is needed to kindle this flame. The glance of a child of genius at an Etruscan vase leaves the child a new being. That is why museums exist: not only for the million who get something from them, but for the one young person of intelligence to whom they mean everything.

Our American universities exhibit very vividly all the signs of retardation in culture, which are traceable in other parts of our social life. A university is always a stronghold of the past, and is therefore one of the last places to be captured by new influence. Commerce has been our ruler for many years; and yet it is only quite recently that the philosophy of commerce can be seen in our colleges. The business man is not a monster; but he is a person who desires to advance his own interests. This is his occupation and, as it were, his religion. The advancement of material interests constitutes civilization to him. He unconsciously infuses the ideas and methods of business into anything that he touches. It has thus come about in America that our universities are beginning to be run as business colleges. They advertise, they compete with each other, they pretend to give good value to their customers. They desire to increase their trade, they offer social advantages and business openings to their patrons. In some cases they boldly conduct intelligence offices, and guarantee that no hard work done by the student shall be done in vain: a record of work is kept during the student's college life, and the college undertakes to furnish him at any time thereafter with references and a character which shall help him in the struggle for life.

This miscarriage of education has been developed and is being conducted by some of our greatest educators, through a perfectly unconscious adaptation of their own souls to the spirit of the age. The underlying philosophy of these men might be stated as follows: "There is nothing in life nobler than for a man to improve his condition and the condition of his children. Learning is a means to this end." Such is the current American conception of education. How far we have departed from the idea of education as a search for truth, or as the vehicle of spiritual expression, may be seen herein. The change of creeds has come about innocently, and the consequences involved in it are, as yet, perceived by hardly anyone. The scepticism inherent in the new creed is concealed by its benevolence. You wish to help the American youth. This unfortunate, benighted, ignorant boy, who has from his cradle heard of nothing but business success as the one goal of all human effort, turns to you for instruction. He comes to you in a trusting spirit, with reverence in his heart, and you answer his hope in this wise: "Business and social success are the best things that life affords. Come to us, my dear fellow, and we will help you toward them." Your son asks you for bread and you give him a stone, for fish and you give him a serpent. It would have been better for that boy if he had never come to your college, for in that case he might have retained a belief that somewhere in the world there existed ideas, art, enthusiasm, unselfishness, inspiring activity.

Learning

In so far as our universities have been turning into business agencies, they have naturally lost their imaginative importance. Our professors seem to be of little more consequence in the community than the department managers of other large shops. If learning is a useful commodity which is to be distributed for the personal advantage of the recipients, it is a thing to be paid for rather than to be worshiped. To be sure, the whole of past history cannot be swept away in a day, and we have not wholly discarded a certain conventional and rhetorical reverence for learning. A dash and varnish of education are thought to be desirable,—the wash that is growing every year more thin.

Now, the truth is that the higher education does not advance a man's personal interests except under special circumstances. What it gives a man is the power of expression; but the ability to express himself has kept many a man poor. Let no one imagine that society is likely to reward him for self-expression in any walk of life. He is much more likely to be punished for it. The question of a man's success in life depends upon society at large. The more highly an age is educated, the more highly it rewards education in the individual. In an age of indifference to learning, the educated man is at a disadvantage. Thus the thesis that education advances self-interest—that thesis upon which many of our colleges are now being conducted—is substantially false. The little scraps and snatches of true education which a man now gets at college often embarrass his career. Our people are finding this out year by year, and as they do so, they naturally throw the true conception of the higher education overboard. If education is to break down as a commercial asset, what excuse have they for retaining it at all? They will force the colleges to live up to the advertisements and to furnish the kind of education that pays its way. It is clear that if the colleges persist in the utilitarian view, the higher learning will disappear. It has been disappearing very rapidly, and can be restored only through the birth of a new spirit and of a new philosophic attitude in our university life.

There are ages when the scholar receives recognition during his lifetime and when the paths which lead to his lecture-room are filled with men drawn there by his fame. This situation arises in any epoch when human intellect surges up and asserts itself against tyranny and ignorance. In the past the tyrannies have been political tyrannies, and these have become well understood through the struggles of intellect in the past; but the present commercial tyranny is a new thing and as yet little understood. It lies like a heavy fog of intellectual depression over the whole kingdom of Mammon, and is fed by the smoke from a million factories. The artist works in it, the thinker thinks in it. Even the saint is born in it. The rain of ashes from the nineteenth-century Vesuvius of business seems to be burying all our landscape.

And yet this is not true. We shall emerge: even we who are in America and suffer most. The important points to be watched are our university class-rooms. If our colleges will but allow something unselfish, something that is true for its own sake, something that is part of the history of the human heart and intellect, to live in their class-rooms, the boys will find their way to it. The museum holds the precious urn, to preserve it. The university, in like manner, stands to house the alphabets of civilization—the historic instruments and agencies of intellect. They are all akin to each other as the very name and function of the place imply. The presidents and professors who sit beside the fountains of knowledge bear different labels and teach subjects that are called by various names. But the thing which carries the label is no more than the shell. The life you cannot label; and it is to foster this life that universities exist. Enthusiasm comes out of the world and goes into the university. Toward this point flow the currents of new talent that bubble up in society: here is the meeting-place of mind. All that a university does is to give the poppy-seed to the soil, the oil to the lamp, the gold to the rod of glass before it cools. A university brings the spirit in touch with its own language, that language through which it has spoken in former days and through which alone it shall speak again.

[1910]

The Function of a University

Youth is not sordid; and the use of a university is that it adds a few years to a man's boyhood, during which his relations to others are not sordid. The problems of life boil down to the question whether one shall be of service to people or shall make use of them; and it makes a great difference whether a man gets his first taste of the issue at the age of 18 or of 22. It makes a great difference, too, whether the intervening years are spent in a counting house, where the very clocks measure nothing but interest, and where the duty to self is preached and practiced at the young man till he feels his nature stiffening into an heroic determination to master this grim and terrible religion of money, or whether those years shall be spent amid surroundings that may awaken the youth to a noble ambition. You may refuse to send your son to a university, you may refuse to have a library in your house, but you cannot greatly disparage the instructive wisdom of mankind which maintains both. There is a utility in them deeper than your cavil. They are perpetual fonts of inspiration for such as know how to use them.

The college buildings, the professors, the games, the societies and the library are a palace of vision. Nothing is spared that can assist vision. The grounds are studded with camerae obscurae showing views of life. But the meaning of these sights is to come afterwards.

If a man is a student while in college he learns to value the accomplishments of valor and intellect; but the cost of them cannot be learned here. The cost remains as unknown as the other side of the moon; language cannot express it. And whether he is a student or not, he lives in an atmosphere of generosity while his bones are setting, and goes out from the place with an integrity which he can, perhaps, never entirely unlearn.

Any one who visits a university feels the influence of a delightful and slightly enervating calm which creeps over him as he crosses the campus. Here are peaceful days and early hours, precision, routine, social happiness. The pictures which the instructors are putting into the slide seem too bright. The instructors themselves appear not to know what tragedies they are handling. The visitor feels he must take the rod from the proctor's hand and give a lecture on the almost imperceptible vestiges of pain still shown on the plate. But the bell rings and it is lunch time. The class in algebra goes on at two.

The lack of vigor in the air of a university comes from the professors. It is impossible for a man to remain at the top of his bent while he is doing anything else but wrestle with new truth; and the temptation of a teacher towards lassitude is overwhelming. He is beyond the reach of new experience, except as he makes it himself in contact with his students and his Faculty; and the man who can make spiritual progress with this outfit is a rare man. The consequence is that most professors go on thinking and teaching the same thing year after year. Give a professor a false thesis in early life, and he will teach it till he dies. He has no way of correcting it.

The rise and progress of new ideas is somewhat as follows: A man makes a discovery; he divulges a theology, or a theory of science or government. If his theory falls into harmony with the current thought of the age, it becomes popular and is taken up on all sides. Years may elapse before a man's theory is adopted

The Function of a University 95

by the world at large as being in harmony with accepted notions, and altogether a plausible thing. But when the day of its popularity arrives and no one is any longer afraid of the doctrine, when it is recognized as useful and at any rate as innocuous, then it is adopted by the learned, and professors are established to teach it in the universities, where it smolders and dies away unless it is reinforced from the world. The master minds of the world, whose thoughts have survived change, thus get set before the young of each generation and together with this valuable heritage of thought, mixed in with it, accepted with the same reverence and transmitted with the same zeal, we find all the not-yet-exploded dogmas of contemporary politics, society and trade.

Such were the reflections that passed through my mind as I turned over the journals on a book stall, and noted the flood of essays upon international politics which the professors in our fresh water colleges have recently been pouring upon the world. It is a striking fact that our college professors of economics have been furnishing the arguments for the imperialists. The learning of the land seems to be given over to a crude and bloodthirsty materialism. It is impossible not to be shocked at the heartless rubbish put forth in the name of science, and embellished with absurd technical terms, by men who know as much about war and government as the spinsters and knitters in the sun who weave their thread with bones. The ferocity of these professors puzzled me greatly till I remembered the explanation of it, and then I perceived that these dominies were the mouthpieces of an academic dogma, and were no more to be blamed than their predecessors who had preached infant damnation, no-faith-with-heretics, or any other orthodoxy that was once so canonized by the world as to be regarded as science by a university.

The cause in all such cases must be sought in history. The early formulation of Darwin's discoveries was coeval with an era of great commercial progress. The phrase "struggle for existence," could be understood by everyone, and seemed to justify any form of self-interest. It became popular at once, was labeled science, was widely accepted, and finally it sifted through into the universities where it is taught to-day. It represents a misapprehension of 1850.

The ideal of a university is to encourage thought. But it is a law of nature that thought cannot move forward except through action. Therefore, a university is no sifting place, but only a treasury. It preserves so much that is really sacred that we can forgive the sanctity it sheds on some ever-changing dross that is shoveled into it and out of it by every passing age. Scientific and prophetic light reaches the university mind thirty years late. Successive dogmas shine down through the elm trees upon leisure and breed pedantry. The pleasant lanes are charged with latent death that makes our pulse beat slower: the lotus is in bloom. We enjoy it for an afternoon and then we cry out "Certainly, this is no place for a grown man." And yet certainly there are no places where grown men are more needed than at the colleges, for the difficulty with these pools of life is to keep open the channels by which the thoughts and feelings of the current world shall run into them.

A thousand new faiths are now forming in the people of the United States; new religions, new forms of spiritual force, and yet such is the constitution of society that they must have passed through the experimental stage before the learned can take note of them. This is due in part to that hiatus in the history of culture which left the mediaeval world at the mercy of the past, and which still stamps all our minds with the instinct that what is of value must be old. It is due in part to the hiatus in our own thought which makes us divide the process of learning from the process of teaching, as if a teacher could have anything more valuable to impart than his own passion to learn the truth. To get professors into your university who want to learn and who have nothing to teach is the way to bring the students as near as possible to the best influences they will meet when they leave your doors. Our western universities have taken a most notable step in filling their chairs of sociology with the younger kind of experimenters. It is true that the torch of the prophet is apt to go out if brought into carbonic acid gas, but on the other hand, the prophet is apt to throw open windows and impart oxygen by which he and all his colleagues may be kept alive. A university ought to be the mere residence of a lot of men who are excited about various aspects of life and history, and who lecture as a means of expressing themselves and of developing their own thought. Their chief corporate bond should be a distrust of each other's society, lest that society come between them and the world. Their great danger is the fixity of their salary and of their entourage, the danger lest this fixity extend itself imperceptibly over their minds. Where such men lived no poppy would bloom, no nerves would grow limp, and the pictures they showed to the young would have in them some tinge of effort and of pain which would imprint them indelibly, and make them hold their own beside the sombre originals which the youth are sure to see at no distant time.

[1900]

Professorial Ethics

When I was at a university as an undergraduate—I will not say how many years ago—I received one morning a visit from a friend who was an upper classman; for, as I remember it, I was a freshman at the time. My friend brought a petition, and wished to interest me in the case of a tutor or assistant professor, a great favorite with the college boys, who was about to be summarily dismissed. There were, to be sure, vague charges against him of incompetence and insubordination; but of the basis of these charges his partisans knew little. They only felt that one of the bright spots in undergraduate life surrounded this same tutor; they liked him and they valued his teaching. I remember no more about this episode, nor do I even remember whether I signed the petition or not. The only thing I very clearly recall is the outcome: the tutor was dismissed.

Twice or thrice again during my undergraduate life, did the same thing happen—a flurry among the students, a remonstrance much too late, against a deed of apparent injustice, a cry in the night, and then silence. Now, had I known more about the world, I should have understood that these nocturnal disturbances were signs of the times, that what we had heard in all these cases was the operation of the guillotine which exists in every American institution of learning, and runs fast or slow according to the progress of the times. The thing that a little astonished the undergraduate at the time was that in almost every case of summary decapitation the victim was an educated gentleman. And this was not because no other kind of man could be found in the faculty. It seemed as if some whimsical fatality hung over the professorial career of any ingenuous gentleman who was by nature a scholar of the charming, old-fashioned kind.

Youth grieves not long over mysterious injustice, and it never occurred to me till many years afterward that there was any logical connection between one and another of all these judicial murders which used to claim a passing tear from the undergraduate at Harvard. It is only since giving some thought to recent educational conditions in America, that I have understood what was then happening, and why it was that a scholar could hardly live in an American University.

In America, society has been reorganized since 1870; the old universities have been totally changed and many new ones founded. The money to do this has come from the business world. The men chosen to do the work have been chosen by the business world. Of a truth, it must needs be that offenses come; but woe be unto him through whom the offense cometh. As the Boss has been the tool of the business man in politics, so the College president has been his agent in education. The colleges during this epoch have each had a "policy" and a directorate. They have been manned and commissioned for a certain kind of service, as you might man a fishing-smack to catch herring. There has been so much necessary business—the business of expanding and planning, of adapting and remodeling—that there has been no time for education. Some big deal has always been pending in each college—some consolidation of departments, some annexation of a new world—something so momentous as to make private opinion a nuisance. In this regard the colleges have resembled everything else in America. The colleges have simply not been different from the rest of American life. Let a man express an opinion at a party caucus, or at a railroad directors' meeting, or at a college faculty meeting, and he will find that he is speaking against a predetermined force. What shall we do with such a fellow? Well, if he is old and distinguished, you may suffer him to have his say, and then override him. But if he is young, energetic, and likely to give more trouble, you must eject him with as little fuss as the circumstances will permit.

The educated man has been the grain of sand in the college machine. He has had a horizon of what "ought to be," and he could not help putting in a word and an idea in the wrong place; and so he was thrown out of education in America exactly as he was thrown out of politics in America. I am here speaking about the great general trend of influences since 1870, influences which have been checked in recent years, checked in politics, checked in education, but which it is necessary to understand if we would understand present conditions in education. The men who, during this era, have been chosen to become college presidents have, as a rule, begun life with the ambition of scholars; but their talents for affairs have been developed at the expense of their taste for learning, and they have become hard men. As toward their faculties they have been autocrats, because the age has demanded autocracy here; as toward the millionaire they have been sycophants, because the age has demanded sycophancy here. Meanwhile these same college presidents represent learning to the imagination of the millionaire and to the imagination of the great public. The ignorant millionaire must trust somebody; and whom he trusts he rules. Now if we go one step further in the reasoning, and discover that the millionaire himself has a somewhat exaggerated reverence for the opinions of the great public, we shall see that this whole matter is a coil of influence emanating from the great public, and winding up—and generally winding up very tight—about the necks of our college faculties and professional scholars. The millionaire and the college president are simply middle men, who transmit the pressure from the average citizen to the learned classes. What the average citizen desires to have done in education gets itself accomplished, though the process should involve the extinction of the race of educated gentlemen. The problem before us in America is the unwinding of this "knot intrinsicate" into which our education has become tied, the unwinding of this boa-constrictor of ignorant public opinion which has been strangling and, to some extent, is still strangling our scholars.

I have no categorical solution of the problem, nor do I, to tell the truth, put an absolute faith in any analysis of social forces, even of my own. If I point out one of the strands in the knot as the best strand to begin work on, it is with the consciousness that there are other effectual ways of working, other ways of feeling about the matter that are more profound.

The natural custodians of education in any age are the learned men of the land, including the professors and schoolmasters. Now these men have, at the present time in America, no conception of their responsibility. They are docile under the rule of the promoting college president, and they have a theory of their own function which debars them from militant activity. The average professor in an American college will look on at an act of injustice done to a brother professor by their college president, with the same unconcern as the rabbit who is not attacked watches the ferret pursue his brother up and down through the warren, to predestinate and horrible death. We know, of course, that it would cost the non-attacked rabbit his place to express sympathy for the martyr; and the non-attacked is poor, and has offspring, and hopes of advancement. The non-attacked rabbit would, of course, become a suspect, and a marked man the moment he lifted up his voice in defense of rabbit-rights. Such personal sacrifice seems to be the price paid in this world for doing good of any kind. I am not, however, here raising the question of general ethics; I refer to the philosophical belief, to the special theory of *professorial* ethics, which forbids a professor to protect his colleague. I invite controversy on this subject; for I should like to know what the professors of the country have to say on it. It seems to me that there exists a special prohibitory code, which prevents the college professor from using his reason and his pen as actively as he ought in protecting himself, in pushing his interests, and in enlightening the community about our educational abuses. The professor in America seems to think that self-respect requires silence and discretion on his part. He is too great to descend into the arena. He thinks that by nursing this gigantic reverence for the idea of professordom, such reverence will, somehow, be extended all over society, till the professor becomes a creature of power, of public notoriety, of independent reputation as he is in Germany. In the meantime, the professor is trampled upon, his interests are ignored, he is overworked and underpaid, he is of small social consequence, he is kept at menial employments, and the leisure to do good work is denied him. A change is certainly needed in all of these aspects of the American professor's life. My own opinion is that this change can only come about through the enlightenment of the great public. The public must be appealed to by the professor himself in all ways and upon all occasions. The professor must teach the nation to respect learning and to understand the function and the rights of the learned classes. He must do this through a willingness to speak and to fight for himself. In Germany there is a great public of highly educated, nay of deeply and variously learned people, whose very existence secures pay, protection, and reverence for the scholar. The same is true in France, England, and Italy.

It is the public that protects the professor in Europe. The public alone can protect the professor in America. The proof of this is that any individual learned man in America who becomes known to the public through his books or his discoveries, or his activity in any field of learning or research, is comparatively safe from the guillotine. His position has at least some security, his word some authority. This man has educated the public that trusts him, and he can now protect his more defenseless brethren, if he will. I have often wondered, when listening to the sickening tale of some brutality done by a practical college president to a young instructor, how it had been possible for the eminent men upon the faculty to sit through the operation without a protest. A word from any one of them would have stopped the sacrifice, and protected learning from the oppressor. But no, these eminent men harbored ethical conceptions which kept them from interfering with the practical running of the college. Merciful heavens! who is to run a college if not learned men? Our colleges have been handled by men whose ideals were as remote from scholarship as the ideals of the New York theatrical managers are remote from poetry. In the meanwhile, the scholars have been dumb and reticent.

At the back of all these phenomena we have, as I have said, the general atmospheric ignorance of the great public in America. We are so used to this public, so immersed in it, so much a part of it ourselves, that we are hardly able to gain any conception of what that atmospheric ignorance is like. I will give an illustration which would perhaps never have occurred to my mind except through the accident of actual experience. If you desire a clue to the American in the matter of the higher education, you may find one in becoming a school trustee in any country district where the children taught are the children of farmers. The contract with any country school-teacher provides that he shall teach for so many weeks, upon such and such conditions. Now let us suppose a teacher of genius to obtain the post. He not only teaches admirably, but he institutes school gardens for the children; he takes long walks with the boys, and gives them the rudiments of geology. He is in himself an uplifting moral influence, and introduces the children into a whole new world of idea and of feeling. The parents are pleased. I will not say that they are grateful; but they are not ungrateful. It is true that they secretly believe all this botany and moral influence to be rubbish; but they tolerate it. Now, let us suppose that before the year is out the teacher falls sick, and loses two weeks of school time through absence. You will find that the trustees insist upon his making up this lost time; the contract calls for it. This seems like a mean and petty exaction for these parents to impose upon a saint who has blessed their children, unto the third and fourth generation, by his presence among them. But let us not judge hastily. This strange exaction does not result so much from the meanness of the parents, as from their intellectual limitations. To these parents the hours passed in school are schooling; the rest does not count. The rest may be pleasant and valuable, but it is not education.

In the same way, the professional and business classes in America do not see any point in paying salaries to professors who are to make researches, or write books, or think beautiful thoughts. The influence which an eminent man sheds about him by his very existence, the change in tone that comes over a rude person through his once seeing the face of a scholar, the illumination of a young character through contact with its own ideals—such things are beyond the ken of the average American citizen to-day. To him, they are fables, to him they are foolishness. The parent of our college lad is a farmer compared to the parent of the European lad.

The American parent regards himself as an enlightened being—yet he has not, in these matters, an inkling of what enlightenment is. Now, the intelligence of that parent must be reached; and the learned classes must do the work of reaching it. The Fathers of the Christian church made war with book and speech on Paganism. The leaders of the Reformation went out among the people and made converts. The patriots of the American Revolution—nay, the fathers of modern science, Tyndal, Huxley, Louis Agaziz, Helmholtz—wrote popular books and sought to interest and educate the public by direct contact. Then let the later-coming followers in learning imitate this popular activity of the old leaders: we need a host of battlers for the cause.

For whom do these universities exist, after all? Is it not for the people at large? Are not the people the ultimate beneficiaries? Then why should the people not be immediately instructed in such manner as will lead to their supporting true universities? It is hard to say why our professors are so timid. Perhaps too great a specialization in their own education has left them helpless, as all-around fighters. But the deeper reason seems to be a moral one; they think such activity is beneath them. It is not beneath them. Whatever be a man's calling, it is not beneath him to make a fight for the truth. As for a professor's belonging to a mystic guild, no man's spiritual force is either increased or diminished by the name he calls his profession. Learning is their cause, and every honest means to promote learning should be within their duty. Nor does duty alone make this call for publicity. Ambition joins in it; the legitimate personal ambition of making one's mind and character felt in the world. This blow once struck means honor, and security of tenure in office, it means public power.

In fine, the scholars should take the public into their confidence and dominate the business men on our college boards. This will be found more easy than at first appears, because the money element, the millionaire element, is very sensitive to public feeling, and once the millionaire succumbs, the college president will succumb also. The step beyond this would consist in the scholars' taking charge of the colleges themselves, merely making use of certain business men on their boards for purposes of financial administration.

[1910]

Greek as a Pleasure

I know not how it may be with other men, but to me, poetical translations of the Greek tragedians have ever been one of the disappointments and annoyances of life. The great reputations of the originals stand out as a never-dying taunt and challenge, luring on the adventurous soul. As he approaches the Greek text, these poetical versions pounce forward upon him, seize, bewilder, fatigue and out-weary him with their thousand-fold flounces and flappings of literary contrivance. They dance like gypsies and pose like models, till he retires to his tent in disgust—retires miles and miles away, to his rightful avocation, to family life, politics and modern literature. Then again, it may be years later, on some fine day his attention is again caught by the looming Colossi afar off behind the huts of the preposterous scholars, and again he glances towards Aeschylus, Sophocles, Euripides.

Now there is a mean, sneaking, and despised band of hackmen, who, for a few pence stand ready to give one a near view of the great figures. I mean the literal translators, and formerly these honest villains would really bring one up to the great creatures and show one something of their anatomy. To be sure, you were not in good society while with the Bohns—you were not in literature, but you got a whiff and inkling that was of mighty interest; you got a Greek feeling, a gritty taste of truth; you could imagine the poetic form as readily as you could imagine the theatrical setting. I have noticed with alarm in more recent years, a growing tendency of the universities to suborn these useful hacks and to dress them in belles lettres. The varlets now wear shirt frills. The good old tramp translators are going out; and the Colossi are being enclosed by a syndicate of impenetrable literary ambition. It is a vain solace to remember Edward Fitzgerald and Gilbert Murray—and if you will, Browning, Swinburne, Matthew Arnold and the other translators of genius, who have enriched the English language with transfusions of amazing beauty, drawn from the Greek. The value of such men is a value added to modern life and to English literature. It all tends to advertise, yet to obscure, the Greek. They are in an unconscious conspiracy to befool the world with new sorceries, and to enclose the oracles with an interpretation so dazzling and so engaging as to balk the curiosity of half the world.

When I made this discovery, I determined to learn Greek, or at any rate to read Greek by the light of every facility except literature—a little of it anyway—a play, half a play, a speech, a couplet—something that was in itself the thing I sought, and not a rendering of it. I had recourse to the garret of memory and there I found a small seedbag of moldy Greek, and with this I began experiments. On reëxamining the first readers and easy grammars which my whole generation had been put through, it seemed to me that they were admirable primers. None need be better. Then why did I not know Greek? The reason was that I had never followed up the beginnings. I had never read a page of Greek out of natural curiosity, nor had I ever seen anyone else do such a thing as to read Greek for pleasure. If anyone will read ten pages of English in the manner in which the schoolboy is taught Greek, he will see why Greek is dropped by the boy as soon as possible. Let anyone analyze ten pages of English, answer grammatical questions upon it, let him be asked to parse and give the parts of irregular verbs, to distinguish between varieties of subjunctive, and he will begin to loathe English literature. For some deep psychological reason the best books to construe are often dull books. Perhaps an amusing book might distract the student's attention. Caesar's Commentaries is the dullest book in Latin. It is like making a road to read it. It is not a book; it is a stone-crushing machine. The teacher, a two-dollar-a-day man, stands beside the machine and runs it. And this is the Classics.

It may be asked, At what point should the reading for pleasure begin? It should begin at about the second lesson, when some entertaining sentence or verse should be learned—as the Lorelei is learned on the first day of German. A little of the language should be put in alive into the child's mind each day; and the grammar should then come behind and sweep up, and explain; it should be kept as a necessary utensil. This relationship should be maintained throughout life; and the attention should be kept on the meanings which occur in sentences and verses, rather than on the shadows of them which the grammars have worked out. The reason why the cart is put before the horse in classical education is that the grammarians through whose admirable labors it is that we possess the classics at all, have always been interested in the cart. It has been their province to study out a rule; and they have interposed this rule between us and the language. They have done it with the best intentions.

There is another circumstance which largely accounts for our inherited misteaching of Latin and Greek. The learned world has been digging out the classics for the last four hundred years; and the ideals of the learned world are accurate scholarship and scientific precision. It is probably right that the learned world should have such ideals—or should have had them during this epoch. And yet accurate scholarship and scientific precision are illusions in the case of language, and there is no scholar living who could write a page of Greek without making ludicrous errors—errors of the sort that the Anglo-Indian makes in writing English, which he has learned from books. If even Mr. Mackail or Gilbert Murray or Nauck, that great, horrible mythic monster—should spend a whole day in dove-tailing phrases which they had fished out of Plato or Thucydides to make an essay of, the chances are that any Athenian would laugh five times to the page over the performance.

If the whole subject were dealt with more lightly, if Greek were treated as, say, French is treated by Frenchmen and Italian by Italians, hundreds of boys would learn Greek with delight and read it easily all their lives, progressing from the simpler authors to the more difficult ones as one goes from Aesop to Thucydides. The whole parade of accuracy should be deliberately subordinated, and allowed to take its rank in each pupil's mind according to his ambition, destination and disposition. If a boy is going to become a teacher of Greek he must take the grammar seriously, but if he only wants to read Greek as he reads French he can get on with a very distant salute to many charming questions.

There should be a great Reader in large print, made up of bits and fragments—dotes, verses, scenes from the dramatists, fragments of Plutarch, Homer and Herodotus. And the boys should be encouraged to read in this book small bits at a time, and easy bits first. And the teacher should be satisfied when the sense is understood and should push the boys on to read and to read, and not to bother about the grammar. Enough grammar will filter into them by degrees to make them understand the constructions—and what else is grammar for? Let the tutor have no ambition to make the boys write Greek. The desire to write Greek is an exotic thing. If a boy has it, let him be encouraged, of course; but let it not be forced upon the next boy. As a matter of fact, the best way to learn to write any language is to read plenty of it; to learn fragments by heart, and fill the mind with the sound of it; then to write it by ear; and thereafter to work up the grammar in correcting what has been written. This is the way to learn French or German; why not Greek? Language is a thing of the ear, and is most easily learned by the ear, and in quantities. Let the children have more Greek, and ever more Greek, and let grammar and critical analysis be kept for dessert.

When one thinks of the thousands of teachers who are obliged to plod year after year through the same portions of Xenophon and Virgil and through the same scenes of Homer, just because of the fear of the Learned World lest the boys should learn the wrong kind of Greek—when one sees the stunting of intelligence, the deadening of interest that must come from such a process—one does not wonder at the decay of Greek in our universities. We have been doing what is hard; we ought to do what is easy.

This long preface may introduce a few brief remarks upon the pleasure and instruction a man may get from a language which he understands in an imperfect, self-taught way. A person who knows, or thinks he knows, no Latin may experience this pleasure by looking over a collection of Latin phrases and proverbs. His brain is fed and transformed by a new stimulus. No one need apologize for attacking the classics in the spirit of amateur curiosity. It was in this manner that Goethe read them. Nor need we believe that their gifts and their instructions are poured out in proportion to the accuracy of the recipient's education in grammar. There are fountains which are closed through the study of grammar as well as fountains which are opened. A belief in the importance of grammar often acts as a grating between mind and literature. There is, to be quite frank, a certain amount of humbug about all grammar. This was true in the time of Protagoras and Aristotle, and became more true as the study was more seriously pursued in the Alexandrine epoch, and as the hardy scholars began to erect wire nettings in the window frames fronting the landscapes of literature.

The modern science of grammar, which is based upon a mediaeval edition of Alexandrine conceptions, seems to have lost none of the rigidity, fussiness and conceit of the Alexandrine epoch. We are obliged to come at Greek poetry through this medium—which did not exist when the poetry was written; but which has been developed and added to, as one of the side products of Western education. Its relation to ancient poetry and to ancient ways of feeling grows falser as time goes on. In the time of the Greek tragedians noun and verb and adjective and conjunction, as we know them, existed not. Greek adjectives are half nouns, pronouns are voices, and might easily be called so; prepositions are moody, bat-like things, and ought probably to be called moods. The verbs turn into nouns upon the slightest provocation, and the case-endings attract and eat each other up with whimsical facility. All is done for the sentiment of the ear, nothing for rule, all is governed by a supergrammatical instinct, which the modern mind can neither practice nor understand. All the words in Greek take their meanings from each other to an extent not easily conceivable. Their wings are in motion like butterflies that will not alight. The air is full of the petals of particles for which we have no modern equivalents and which yet flutter and wheel with an inner poetry and an inimitable logic of their own. We were men before we were scholars, and therefore these things affect us like music.

The grammarian, with his immense cabinet of miniature surgical instruments, attacks this fairyland. He weaves about it a whole underworld of weird, unearthly, morbid wisdom. Grammar is a strange study which clouds the mind like opium. A language is invented, dark and technical, like mediaeval law, like mediaeval theology, an ontological language which moves among half-understood and awesome realities—like Dante in purgatory. It is this gloomy and fascinating tongue which the students learn—a tongue much harder than Greek, and possessing a literature many times as large as classical Greek literature and made up entirely of grammars. This cabalistic language is ever pushed forward by the scholars.

Everything that has ever been written about the Classics has had its influence in bringing us to them. Let us accept all this steering with gratitude, and come into port. Let us shut our guidebooks, and look at the works and fragments of antiquity with all our eyes.

[1913]

Emerson

I

"Leave this hypocritical prating about the masses. Masses are rude, lame, unmade, pernicious in their demands and influence, and need not to be flattered, but to be schooled. I wish not to concede anything to them, but to tame, drill, divide, and break them up, and draw individuals out of them. The worst of charity is that the lives you are asked to preserve are not worth preserving. Masses! The calamity is the masses. I do not wish any mass at all, but honest men only, lovely, sweet, accomplished women only, and no shovel-handed, narrow-brained, gin-drinking million stockingers or lazzaroni at all. If government knew how, I should like to see it check, not multiply the population. When it reaches its true law of action, every man that is born will be hailed as essential. Away with this hurrah of masses, and let us have the considerate vote of single men spoken on their honor and their conscience."

This extract from The Conduct of Life gives fairly enough the leading thought of Emerson's life. The unending warfare between the individual and society shows us in each generation a poet or two, a dramatist or a musician who exalts and deifies the individual, and leads us back again to the only object which is really worthy of enthusiasm or which can permanently excite it,—the character of a man. It is surprising to find this identity of content in all great deliverances. The only thing we really admire is personal liberty. Those who fought for it and those who enjoyed it are our heroes.

But the hero may enslave his race by bringing in a system of tyranny; the battle-cry of freedom may become a dogma which crushes the soul; one good custom may corrupt the world. And so the inspiration of one age becomes the damnation of the next. This crystallizing of life into death has occurred so often that it may almost be regarded as one of the laws of progress.

Emerson represents a protest against the tyranny of democracy. He is the most recent example of elemental hero-worship. His opinions are absolutely unqualified except by his temperament. He expresses a form of belief in the importance of the individual which is independent of any personal relations he has with the world. It is as if a man had been withdrawn from the earth and dedicated to condensing and embodying this eternal idea—the value of the individual soul—so vividly, so vitally, that his words could not die, yet in such illusive and abstract forms that by no chance and by no power could his creed be used for purposes of tyranny. Dogma cannot be extracted from it. Schools cannot be built on it. It either lives as the spirit lives, or else it evaporates and leaves nothing. Emerson was so afraid of the letter that killeth that he would hardly trust his words to print. He was assured there was no such thing as literal truth, but only literal falsehood. He therefore resorted to metaphors which could by no chance be taken literally. And he has probably succeeded in leaving a body of work which cannot be made to operate to any other end than that for which he designed it. If this be true, he has accomplished the inconceivable feat of eluding misconception. If it be true, he stands alone in the history of teachers; he has circumvented fate, he has left an unmixed blessing behind him.

The signs of those times which brought forth Emerson are not wholly undecipherable. They are the same times which gave rise to every character of significance during the period before the war. Emerson is indeed the easiest to understand of all the men of his time, because his life is freest from the tangles and qualifications of circumstance. He is a sheer and pure type and creature of destiny, and the unconsciousness that marks his development allies him to the deepest phenomena. It is convenient, in describing him, to use language which implies consciousness on his part, but he himself had no purpose, no theory of himself; he was a product.

The years between 1820 and 1830 were the most pitiable through which this country has ever passed. The conscience of the North was pledged to the Missouri Compromise, and that Compromise neither slumbered nor slept. In New England, where the old theocratical oligarchy of the colonies had survived the Revolution and kept under its own waterlocks the new flood of trade, the conservatism of politics reinforced the conservatism of religion; and as if these two inquisitions were not enough to stifle the soul of man, the conservatism of business self-interest was superimposed. The history of the conflicts which followed has been written by the radicals, who negligently charge up to self-interest all the resistance which establishments offer to change. But it was not solely self-interest, it was conscience that backed the Missouri Compromise, nowhere else, naturally, so strongly as in New England. It was conscience that made cowards of us all. The white-lipped generation of Edward Everett were victims, one might even say martyrs, to conscience. They suffered the most terrible martyrdom that can fall to man, a martyrdom which injured their immortal volition and dried up the springs of life. If it were not that our poets have too seldom deigned to dip into real life, I do not know what more awful subject for a poem could have been found than that of the New England judge enforcing the fugitive slave law. For lack of such a poem the heroism of these men has been forgotten, the losing heroism of conservatism. It was this spiritual power of a committed conscience which met the new forces as they arose, and it deserves a better name than these new forces afterward gave it. In 1830 the social fruits of these heavy conditions could be seen in the life of the period. Free speech was lost.

"I know no country," says Tocqueville, who was here in 1831, "in which there is so little independence of mind and freedom of discussion as in America." Tocqueville recurs to the point again and again. He cannot disguise his surprise at it, and it tinged his whole philosophy and his book. The timidity of the Americans of this era was a thing which intelligent foreigners could not understand. Miss Martineau wrote in her Autobiography: "It was not till months afterwards that I was told that there were two reasons why I was not invited there [Chelsea] as elsewhere. One reason was that I had avowed, in reply to urgent questions, that I was disappointed in an oration of Mr. Everett's; and another was that I had publicly condemned the institution of slavery. I hope the Boston people have outgrown the childishness of sulking at opinions not in either case volunteered, but obtained by pressure. But really, the subservience to opinion at that time seemed a sort of mania."

The mania was by no means confined to Boston, but qualified this period of our history throughout the Northern States. There was no literature. "If great writers have not at present existed in America, the reason is very simply given in the fact that there can be no literary genius without freedom of opinion, and freedom of opinion does not exist in America," wrote Tocqueville. There were no amusements, neither music nor sport nor pastime, indoors or out of doors. The whole life of the community was a life of the intelligence, and upon the intelligence lay the weight of intellectual tyranny. The pressure kept on increasing, and the suppressed forces kept on increasing, till at last, as if to show what gigantic power was needed to keep conservatism dominant, the Merchant Province put forward Daniel Webster.

The worst period of panic seems to have preceded the antislavery agitations of 1831, because these agitations soon demonstrated that the sky did not fall nor the earth yawn and swallow Massachusetts because of Mr. Garrison's opinions, as most people had sincerely believed would be the case. Some semblance of free speech was therefore gradually regained.

Let us remember the world upon which the young Emerson's eyes opened. The South was a plantation. The North crooked the hinges of the knee where thrift might follow fawning. It was the era of Martin Chuzzlewit, a malicious caricature,—founded on fact. This time of humiliation, when there was no free speech, no literature, little manliness, no reality, no simplicity, no accomplishment, was the era of American brag. We flattered the foreigner and we boasted of ourselves. We were over-sensitive, insolent, and cringing. As late as 1845, G.P. Putnam, a most sensible and modest man, published a book to show what the country had done in the field of culture. The book is a monument of the age. With all its good sense and good humor, it justifies foreign contempt because it is explanatory. Underneath everything lay a feeling of unrest, an instinct,—"this country cannot permanently endure half slave and half free,"—which was the truth, but which could not be uttered.

So long as there is any subject which men may not freely discuss, they are timid upon all subjects. They wear an iron crown and talk in whispers. Such social conditions crush and maim the individual, and throughout New England, as throughout the whole North, the individual was crushed and maimed.

The generous youths who came to manhood between 1820 and 1830, while this deadly era was maturing, seem to have undergone a revulsion against the world almost before touching it; at least two of them suffered, revolted, and condemned, while still boys sitting on benches in school, and came forth advancing upon this old society like gladiators. The activity of William Lloyd Garrison, the man of action, preceded by several years that of Emerson, who is his prophet. Both of them were parts of one revolution. One of Emerson's articles of faith was that a man's thoughts spring from his actions rather than his actions from his thoughts, and possibly the same thing holds good for society at large. Perhaps all truths, whether moral or economic, must be worked out in real life before they are discovered by the student, and it was therefore necessary that Garrison should be evolved earlier than Emerson.

The silent years of early manhood, during which Emerson passed through the Divinity School and to his ministry, known by few, understood by none, least of all by himself, were years in which the revolting spirit of an archangel thought out his creed. He came forth perfect, with that serenity of which we have scarce another example in history,—that union of the man himself, his beliefs, and his vehicle of expression that makes men great because it makes them comprehensible. The philosophy into which he had already transmuted all his earlier theology at the time we first meet him consisted of a very simple drawing together of a few ideas, all of which had long been familiar to the world. It is the wonderful use he made of these ideas, the closeness with which they fitted his soul, the tact with which he took what he needed, like a bird building its nest, that make the originality, the man.

The conclusion of Berkeley, that the external world is known to us only through our impressions, and that therefore, for aught we know, the whole universe exists only in our own consciousness, cannot be disproved. It is so simple a conception that a child may understand it; and it has probably been passed before the attention of every thinking man since Plato's time. The notion is in itself a mere philosophical catch or crux to which there is no answer. It may be true. The mystics made this doctrine useful. They were not content to doubt the independent existence of the external world. They imagined that this external world, the earth, the planets, the phenomena of nature, bore some relation to the emotions and destiny of the soul. The soul and the cosmos were somehow related, and related so intimately that the cosmos might be regarded as a sort of projection or diagram of the soul.

Plato was the first man who perceived that this idea could be made to provide the philosopher with a vehicle of expression more powerful than any other. If a man will once plant himself firmly on the proposition that *he is* the universe, that every emotion or expression of his mind is correlated in some way to phenomena in the external world, and that he shall say how correlated, he is in a position where the power of speech is at a maximum. His figures of speech, his tropes, his witticisms, take rank with the law of gravity and the precession of the equinoxes. Philosophical exaltation of the individual cannot go beyond this point. It is the climax.

This is the school of thought to which Emerson belonged. The sun and moon, the planets, are mere symbols. They signify whatever the poet chooses. The planets for the most part stay in conjunction just long enough to flash his thought through their symbolism, and no permanent relation is established between the soul and the zodiac. There is, however, one link of correlation between the external and internal worlds which Emerson considered established, and in which he believed almost literally, namely, the moral law. This idea he drew from Kant through Coleridge and Wordsworth, and it is so familiar to us all that it hardly needs stating. The fancy that the good, the true, the beautiful,—all things of which we instinctively approve,—are somehow connected together and are really one thing; that our appreciation of them is in its essence the recognition of a law; that this law, in fact all law and the very idea of law, is a mere subjective experience; and that hence any external sequence which we coördinate and name, like the law of gravity, is really intimately connected with our moral nature,— this fancy has probably some basis of truth. Emerson adopted it as a corner-stone of his thought.

Such are the ideas at the basis of Emerson's philosophy, and it is fair to speak of them in this place because they antedate everything else which we know of him. They had been for years in his mind before he spoke at all. It was in the armor of this invulnerable idealism and with weapons like shafts of light that he came forth to fight.

In 1836, at the age of thirty-three, Emerson published the little pamphlet called Nature, which was an attempt to state his creed. Although still young, he was not without experience of life. He had been assistant minister to the Rev. Dr. Ware from 1829 to 1832, when he resigned his ministry on account of his views regarding the Lord's Supper. He had married and lost his first wife in the same interval. He had been abroad and had visited Carlyle in 1833. He had returned and settled in Concord, and had taken up the profession of lecturing, upon which he in part supported himself ever after. It is unnecessary to review these early lectures. "Large portions of them," says Mr. Cabot, his biographer, "appeared afterwards in the Essays, especially those of the first series." Suffice it that through them Emerson had become so well known that although Nature was published anonymously, he was recognized as the author. Many people had heard of him at the time he resigned his charge, and the story went abroad that the young minister of the Second Church had gone mad. The lectures had not discredited the story, and Nature seemed to corroborate it. Such was the impression which the book made upon Boston in 1836. As we read it to-day, we are struck by its extraordinary beauty of language. It is a supersensuous, lyrical, and sincere rhapsody, written evidently by a man of genius. It reveals a nature compelling respect,—a Shelley, and yet a sort of Yankee Shelley, who is mad only when the wind is nor'-nor'west; a mature nature which must have been nourished for years upon its own thoughts, to speak this new language so eloquently, to stand so calmly on its feet. The deliverance of his thought is so perfect that this work adapts itself to our mood and has the quality of poetry. This fluency Emerson soon lost; it is the quality missing in his poetry. It is the efflorescence of youth.

"In good health, the air is a cordial of incredible virtue. Crossing a bare common, in snow puddles, at twilight, under a clouded sky, without having in my thoughts any occurrence of special good fortune, I have enjoyed a perfect exhilaration. I am glad to the brink of fear. In the woods, too, a man casts off his years, as the snake his slough, and at what period soever of life is always a child. In the woods is perpetual youth. Within these plantations of God, a decorum and sanctity reign, a perennial festival is dressed, and the guest sees not how he should tire of them in a thousand years. . . . It is the uniform effect of culture on the human mind, not to shake our faith in the stability of particular phenomena, as heat, water, azote; but to lead us to regard nature as phenomenon, not a substance; to attribute necessary existence to spirit; to esteem nature as an accident and an effect."

Perhaps these quotations from the pamphlet called Nature are enough to show the clouds of speculation in which Emerson had been walking. With what lightning they were charged was soon seen.

In 1837 he was asked to deliver the Phi Beta Kappa oration at Cambridge. This was the opportunity for which he had been waiting. The mystic and eccentric young poet-preacher now speaks his mind, and he turns out to be a man exclusively interested in real life. This recluse, too tender for contact with the rough facts of the world, whose conscience has retired him to rural Concord, pours out a vial of wrath. This cub puts forth the paw of a full-grown lion.

Emerson has left behind him nothing stronger than this address, The American Scholar. It was the first application of his views to the events of his day, written and delivered in the heat of early manhood while his extraordinary powers were at their height. It moves with a logical progression of which he soon lost the habit. The subject of it, the scholar's relation to the world, was the passion of his life. The body of his belief is to be found in this address, and in any adequate account of him the whole address ought to be given.

"Thus far," he said, "our holiday has been simply a friendly sign of the survival of the love of letters amongst a people too busy to give to letters any more. As such it is precious as the sign of an indestructible instinct. Perhaps the time is already come when it ought to be, and will be, something else; when the sluggard intellect of this continent will look from under its iron lids and fill the postponed expectation of the world with something better than the exertions of mechanical skill. . . . The theory of books is noble. The scholar of the first age received into him the world around; brooded thereon; gave it the new arrangement of his own mind, and uttered it again. It came into him life; it went out from him truth.... Yet hence arises a grave mischief. The sacredness which attaches to the act of creation, the act of thought, is transferred to the record. The poet chanting was felt to be a divine man: henceforth the chant is divine, also. The writer was a just and wise spirit: henceforward it is settled the book is perfect; as love of the hero corrupts into worship of his statue. Instantly the book becomes noxious: the guide is a tyrant.... Books are the best of things, well used; abused, among the worst. What is the right use? What is the one end which all means go to effect? They are for nothing but to inspire.... The one thing in the world, of value, is the active soul. This every man is entitled to; this every man contains within him, although in almost all men obstructed, and as yet unborn. The soul active sees absolute truth and utters truth, or creates. In this action it is genius; not the privilege of here and there a favorite, but the sound estate of every man.... Genius is always sufficiently the enemy of genius by over-influence. The literature of every nation bears me witness. The English dramatic poets have Shakespearized now for two hundred years.... These being his functions, it becomes him to feel all confidence in himself, and to defer never to the popular cry. He, and he only, knows the world. The world of any moment is the merest appearance. Some great decorum, some fetish of a government, some ephemeral trade, or war, or man, is cried up by half mankind and cried down by the other half, as if all depended on this particular up or down. The odds are that the whole question is not worth the poorest thought which the scholar has lost in listening to the controversy. Let him not quit his belief that a popgun is a popgun, though the ancient and honorable of the earth affirm it to be the crack of doom."

Dr. Holmes called this speech of Emerson's our "intellectual Declaration of Independence," and indeed it was. "The Phi Beta Kappa speech," says Mr. Lowell, "was an event without any former parallel in our literary annals,—a scene always to be treasured in the memory for its picturesqueness and its inspiration. What crowded and breathless aisles, what windows clustering with eager heads, what enthusiasm of approval, what grim silence of foregone dissent!"

The authorities of the Divinity School can hardly have been very careful readers of Nature and The American Scholar, or they would not have invited Emerson, in 1838, to deliver the address to the graduating class. This was Emerson's second opportunity to apply his beliefs directly to society. A few lines out of the famous address are enough to show that he saw in the church of his day signs of the same decadence that he saw in the letters: "The prayers and even the dogmas of our church are like the zodiac of Denderah and the astronomical monuments of the Hindoos, wholly insulated from anything now extant in the life and business of the people. They mark the height to which the waters once rose.... It is the office of a true teacher to show us that God is, not was; that he speaketh, not spake. The true Christianity—a faith like Christ's in the infinitude of man—is lost. None believeth in the soul of man, but only in some man or person old and departed. Ah me! no man goeth alone. All men go in flocks to this saint or that poet, avoiding the God who seeth in secret. They cannot see in secret; they love to be blind in public. They think society wiser than their soul, and know not that one soul, and their soul, is wiser than the whole world."

It is almost misleading to speak of the lofty utterances of these early addresses as attacks upon society, but their reception explains them. The element of absolute courage is the same in all natures. Emerson himself was not unconscious of what function he was performing.

The "storm in our wash-bowl" which followed this Divinity School address, the letters of remonstrance from friends, the advertisements by the Divinity School of "no complicity," must have been cheering to Emerson. His unseen yet dominating ambition is shown throughout the address, and in this note in his diary of the following year:—

"*August* 31. Yesterday at the Phi Beta Kappa anniversary. Steady, steady. I am convinced that if a man will be a true scholar he shall have perfect freedom. The young people and the mature hint at odium and the aversion of forces to be presently encountered in society. I say No; I fear it not."

The lectures and addresses which form the latter half of the first volume in the collected edition show the early Emerson in the ripeness of his powers. These writings have a lyrical sweep and a beauty which the later works often lack. Passages in them remind us of Hamlet:—

"How silent, how spacious, what room for all, yet without space to insert an atom;—in graceful succession, in equal fulness, in balanced beauty, the dance of the hours goes forward still. Like an odor of incense, like a strain of music, like a sleep, it is inexact and boundless. It will not be dissected, nor unravelled, nor shown.... The great Pan of old, who was clothed in a leopard skin to signify the beautiful variety of things and the firmament, his coat of stars,—was but the representative of thee, O rich and various man! thou palace of sight and sound, carrying in thy senses the morning and the night and the unfathomable galaxy; in thy brain, the geometry of the City of God; in thy heart, the bower of love and the realms of right and wrong.... Every star in heaven is discontent and insatiable. Gravitation and chemistry cannot content them. Ever they woo and court the eye of the beholder. Every man who comes into the world they seek to fascinate and possess, to pass into his mind, for they desire to republish themselves in a more delicate world than that they occupy.... So it is with all immaterial objects. These beautiful basilisks set their brute glorious eyes on the eye of every child, and, if they can, cause their nature to pass through his wondering eyes into him, and so all things are mixed."

Emerson is never far from his main thought:—

"The universe does not attract us till it is housed in an individual."

"A man, a personal ascendency, is the only great phenomenon."

"I cannot find language of sufficient energy to convey my sense of the sacredness of private integrity."

On the other hand, he is never far from his great fear: "But Truth is such a fly-away, such a sly-boots, so untransportable and unbarrelable a commodity, that it is as bad to catch as light."

"Let him beware of proposing to himself any end. . . . I say to you plainly, there is no end so sacred or so large that if pursued for itself will not become carrion and an offence to the nostril."

There can be nothing finer than Emerson's knowledge of the world, his sympathy with young men and with the practical difficulties of applying his teachings. We can see in his early lectures before students and mechanics how much he had learned about the structure of society from his own short contact with the organized church.

"Each finds a tender and very intelligent conscience a disqualification for success. Each requires of the practitioner a certain shutting of the eyes, a certain dapperness and compliance, an acceptance of customs, a sequestration from the sentiments of generosity and love, a compromise of private opinion and lofty integrity. . . . The fact that a new thought and hope have dawned in your breast, should apprise you that in the same hour a new light broke in upon a thousand private hearts. . . . And further I will not dissemble my hope that each person whom I address has felt his own call to cast aside all evil customs, timidity, and limitations, and to be in his place a free and helpful man, a reformer, a benefactor, not content to slip along through the world like a footman or a spy, escaping by his nimbleness and apologies as many knocks as he can, but a brave and upright man who must find or cut a straight road to everything excellent in the earth, and not only go honorably himself, but make it easier for all who follow him to go in honor and with benefit. . . ."

Beneath all lay a greater matter,—Emerson's grasp of the forms and conditions of progress, his reach of intellect, which could afford fair play to every one.

His lecture on The Conservative is not a puzzling *jeu d'esprit*, like Bishop Blougram's Apology, but an honest attempt to set up the opposing chessmen of conservatism and reform so as to represent real life. Hardly can such a brilliant statement of the case be found elsewhere in literature. It is not necessary to quote here the reformer's side of the question, for Emerson's whole life was devoted to it. The conservatives' attitude he gives with such accuracy and such justice that the very bankers of State Street seem to be speaking:—

"The order of things is as good as the character of the population permits. Consider it as the work of a great and beneficent and progressive necessity, which, from the first pulsation in the first animal life up to the present high culture of the best nations, has advanced thus far. . . .

"The conservative party in the universe concedes that the radical would talk sufficiently to the purpose if we were still in the garden of Eden; he legislates for man as he ought to be; his theory is right, but he makes no allowance for friction, and this omission makes his whole doctrine false. The idealist retorts that the conservative falls into a far more noxious error in the other extreme. The conservative assumes sickness as a necessity, and his social frame is a hospital, his total legislation is for the present distress, a universe in slippers and flannels, with bib and pap-spoon, swallowing pills and herb tea. Sickness gets organized as well as health, the vice as well as the virtue."

It is unnecessary to go, one by one, through the familiar essays and lectures which Emerson published between 1838 and 1875. They are in everybody's hands and in everybody's thoughts. In 1840 he wrote in his diary: "In all my lectures I have taught one doctrine, namely, the infinitude of the private man. This the people accept readily enough, and even with commendation, as long as I call the lecture Art or Politics, or Literature or the Household; but the moment I call it Religion they are shocked, though it be only the application of the same truth which they receive elsewhere to a new class of facts." To the platform he returned, and left it only once or twice during the remainder of his life.

His writings vary in coherence. In his early occasional pieces, like the Phi Beta Kappa address, coherence is at a maximum. They were written for a purpose, and were perhaps struck off all at once. But he earned his living by lecturing, and a lecturer is always recasting his work and using it in different forms. A lecturer has no prejudice against repetition. It is noticeable that in some of Emerson's important lectures the logical scheme is more perfect than in his essays. The truth seems to be that in the process of working up and perfecting his writings, in revising and filing his sentences, the logical scheme became more and more obliterated. Another circumstance helped make his style fragmentary. He was by nature a man of inspirations and exalted moods. He was subject to ecstasies, during which his mind worked with phenomenal brilliancy. Throughout his works and in his diary we find constant reference to these moods, and to his own inability to control or recover them. "But what we want is consecutiveness. 'T is with us a flash of light, then a long darkness, then a flash again. Ah! could we turn these fugitive sparkles into an astronomy of Copernican worlds!"

In order to take advantage of these periods of divination, he used to write down the thoughts that came to him at such times. From boyhood onward he kept journals and commonplace books, and in the course of his reading and meditation he collected innumerable notes and quotations which he indexed for ready use. In these mines he "quarried," as Mr. Cabot says, for his lectures and essays. When he needed a lecture he went to the repository, threw together what seemed to have a bearing on some subject, and gave it a title. If any other man should adopt this method of composition, the result would be incomprehensible chaos; because most men have many interests, many moods, many and conflicting ideas. But with Emerson it was otherwise. There was only one thought which could set him aflame, and that was the thought of the unfathomed might of man. This thought was his religion, his politics, his ethics, his philosophy. One moment of inspiration was in him own brother to the next moment of inspiration, although they might be separated by six weeks. When he came to put together his star-born ideas, they fitted well, no matter in what order he placed them, because they were all part of the same idea.

His works are all one single attack on the vice of the age, moral cowardice. He assails it not by railings and scorn, but by positive and stimulating suggestion. The imagination of the reader is touched by every device which can awake the admiration for heroism, the consciousness of moral courage. Wit, quotation, anecdote, eloquence, exhortation, rhetoric, sarcasm, and very rarely denunciation, are launched at the reader, till he feels little lambent flames beginning to kindle in him. He is perhaps unable to see the exact logical connection between two paragraphs of an essay, yet he feels they are germane. He takes up Emerson tired and apathetic, but presently he feels himself growing heady and truculent, strengthened in his most inward vitality, surprised to find himself again master in his own house.

The difference between Emerson and the other moralists is that all these simulating pictures and suggestions are not given by him in illustration of a general proposition. They have never been through the mill of generalization in his own mind. He himself could not have told you their logical bearing on one another. They have all the vividness of disconnected fragments of life, and yet they all throw light on one another, like the facets of a jewel. But whatever cause it was that led him to adopt his method of writing, it is certain that he succeeded in delivering himself of his thought with an initial velocity and carrying power such as few men ever attained. He has the force at his command of the thrower of the discus.

His style is American, and beats with the pulse of the climate. He is the only writer we have had who writes as he speaks, who makes no literary parade, has no pretensions of any sort. He is the only writer we have had who has wholly subdued his vehicle to his temperament. It is impossible to name his style without naming his character: they are one thing.

Both in language and in elocution Emerson was a practised and consummate artist, who knew how both to command his effects and to conceal his means. The casual, practical, disarming directness with which he writes puts any honest man at his mercy. What difference does it make whether a man who can talk like this is following an argument or not? You cannot always see Emerson clearly; he is hidden by a high wall; but you always know exactly on what spot he is standing. You judge it by the flight of the objects he throws over the wall,—a bootjack, an apple, a crown, a razor, a volume of verse. With one or other of these missiles, all delivered with a very tolerable aim, he is pretty sure to hit you. These catchwords stick in the mind. People are not in general influenced by long books or discourses, but by odd fragments of observation which they overhear, sentences or head-lines which they read while turning over a book at random or while waiting for dinner to be announced. These are the oracles and orphic words that get lodged in the mind and bend a man's most stubborn will. Emerson called them the Police of the Universe. His works are a treasury of such things. They sparkle in the mine, or you may carry them off in your pocket. They get driven into your mind like nails, and on them catch and hang your own experiences, till what was once his thought has become your character.

"God offers to every mind its choice between truth and repose. Take which you please; you can never have both." "Discontent is want of self-reliance; it is infirmity of will." "It is impossible for a man to be cheated by any one but himself."

The orchestration with which Emerson introduces and sustains these notes from the spheres is as remarkable as the winged things themselves. Open his works at a hazard. You hear a man talking.

"A garden is like those pernicious machineries we read of every month in the newspapers, which catch a man's coat-skirt or his hand, and draw in his arm, his leg, and his whole body to irresistible destruction. In an evil hour he pulled down his wall and added a field to his homestead. No land is bad, but land is worse. If a man own land, the land owns him. Now let him leave home if he dare. Every tree and graft, every hill of melons, row of corn, or quickset hedge, all he has done and all he means to do, stand in his way like duns, when he would go out of his gate."

Your attention is arrested by the reality of this gentleman in his garden, by the first-hand quality of his mind. It matters not on what subject he talks. While you are musing, still pleased and patronizing, he has picked up the bow of Ulysses, bent it with the ease of Ulysses, and sent a shaft clear through the twelve axes, nor missed one of them. But this, it seems, was mere by-play and marksmanship; for before you have done wondering, Ulysses rises to his feet in anger, and pours flight after flight, arrow after arrow, from the great bow. The shafts sing and strike, the suitors fall in heaps. The brow of Ulysses shines with unearthly splendor. The air is filled with lightning. After a little, without shock or transition, without apparent change of tone, Mr. Emerson is offering you a biscuit before you leave, and bidding you mind the last step at the garden end. If the man who can do these things be not an artist, then must we have a new vocabulary and rename the professions.

There is, in all this effectiveness of Emerson, no pose, no literary art; nothing that corresponds even remotely to the pretended modesty and ignorance with which Socrates lays pitfalls for our admiration in Plato's dialogues.

It was the platform which determined Emerson's style. He was not a writer, but a speaker. On the platform his manner of speech was a living part of his words. The pauses and hesitation, the abstraction, the searching, the balancing, the turning forward and back of the leaves of his lecture, and then the discovery, the illumination, the gleam of lightning which you saw before your eyes descend into a man of genius,—all this was Emerson. He invented this style of speaking, and made it express the supersensuous, the incommunicable. Lowell wrote, while still under the spell of the magician: "Emerson's oration was more disjointed than usual, even with him. It began nowhere, and ended everywhere, and yet, as always with that divine man, it left you feeling that something beautiful had passed that way, something more beautiful than anything else, like the rising and setting of stars. Every possible criticism might have been made on it but one,—that it was not noble. There was a tone in it that awakened all elevating associations. He boggled, he lost his place, he had to put on his glasses; but it was as if a creature from some fairer world had lost his way in our fogs, and it was *our* fault, not his. It was chaotic, but it was all such stuff as stars are made of, and you could n't help feeling that, if you waited awhile, all that was nebulous would be whirled into planets, and would assume the mathematical gravity of system. All through it I felt something in me that cried, 'Ha! ha!' to the sound of the trumpets."

It is nothing for any man sitting in his chair to be overcome with the sense of the immediacy of life, to feel the spur of courage, the victory of good over evil, the value, now and forever, of all great-hearted endeavor. Such moments come to us all. But for a man to sit in his chair and write what shall call up these forces in the bosoms of others—that is desert, that is greatness. To do this was the gift of Emerson. The whole earth is enriched by every moment of converse with him. The shows and shams of life become transparent, the lost kingdoms are brought back, the shutters of the spirit are opened, and provinces and realms of our own existence lie gleaming before us.

It has been necessary to reduce the living soul of Emerson to mere dead attributes like "moral courage" in order that we might talk about him at all. His effectiveness comes from his character; not from his philosophy, nor from his rhetoric nor his wit, nor from any of the accidents of his education. He might never have heard of Berkeley or Plato. A slightly different education might have led him to throw his teaching into the form of historical essays or of stump speeches. He might, perhaps, have been bred a stone-mason, and have done his work in the world by travelling with a panorama. But he would always have been Emerson. His weight and his power would always have been the same. It is solely as character that he is important. He discovered nothing; he bears no relation whatever to the history of philosophy. We must regard him and deal with him simply as a man.

Strangely enough, the world has always insisted upon accepting him as a thinker: and hence a great coil of misunderstanding. As a thinker, Emerson is difficult to classify. Before you begin to assign him a place, you must clear the ground by a disquisition as to what is meant by "a thinker," and how Emerson differs from other thinkers. As a man, Emerson is as plain as Ben Franklin.

People have accused him of inconsistency; they say that he teaches one thing one day, and another the next day. But from the point of view of Emerson there is no such thing as inconsistency. Every man is each day a new man. Let him be to-day what he is to-day. It is immaterial and waste of time to consider what he once was or what he may be.

His picturesque speech delights in fact and anecdote, and a public which is used to treatises and deduction cares always to be told the moral. It wants everything reduced to a generalization. All generalizations are partial truths, but we are used to them, and we ourselves mentally make the proper allowance. Emerson's method is, not to give a generalization and trust to our making the allowance, but to give two conflicting statements and leave the balance of truth to be struck in our own minds on the facts. There is no inconsistency in this. It is a vivid and very legitimate method of procedure. But he is much more than a theorist: he is a practitioner. He does not merely state a theory of agitation: he proceeds to agitate. "Do not," he says, "set the least value on what I do, or the least discredit on what I do not, as if I pretended to settle anything as false or true. I unsettle all things. No facts are to me sacred, none are profane. I simply experiment, an endless seeker with no past at my back." He was not engaged in teaching many things, but one thing,—Courage. Sometimes he inspires it by pointing to great characters,—Fox, Milton, Alcibiades; sometimes he inspires it by bidding us beware of imitating such men, and, in the ardor of his rhetoric, even seems to regard them as hindrances and dangers to our development. There is no inconsistency here. Emerson might logically have gone one step further and raised inconsistency into a jewel. For what is so useful, so educational, so inspiring, to a timid and conservative man, as to do something inconsistent and regrettable? It lends character to him at once. He breathes freer and is stronger for the experience.

Emerson is no cosmopolitan. He is a patriot. He is not like Goethe, whose sympathies did not run on national lines. Emerson has America in his mind's eye all the time. There is to be a new religion, and it is to come from America; a new and better type of man, and he is to be an American. He not only cared little or nothing for Europe, but he cared not much for the world at large. His thought was for the future of this country. You cannot get into any chamber in his mind which is below this chamber of patriotism. He loves the valor of Alexander and the grace of the Oxford athlete; but he loves them not for themselves. He has a use for them. They are grist to his mill and powder to his gun. His admiration of them he subordinates to his main purpose,—they are his blackboard and diagrams. His patriotism is the backbone of his significance. He came to his countrymen at a time when they lacked, not thoughts, but manliness. The needs of his own particular public are always before him.

"It is odd that our people should have, not water on the brain, but a little gas there. A shrewd foreigner said of the Americans that 'whatever they say has a little the air of a speech.'"

"I shall not need to go into an enumeration of our national defects and vices which require this Order of Censors in the State.... The timidity of our public opinion is our disease, or, shall I say, the publicness of opinion, the absence of private opinion."

"Our measure of success is the moderation and low level of an individual's judgment. Dr. Channing's piety and wisdom had such weight in Boston that the popular idea of religion was whatever this eminent divine held."

"Let us affront and reprimand the smooth mediocrity, the squalid contentment of the times."

The politicians he scores constantly.

"Who that sees the meanness of our politics but congratulates Washington that he is long already wrapped in his shroud and forever safe." The following is his description of the social world of his day: "If any man consider the present aspects of what is called by distinction *society*, he will see the need of these ethics. The sinew and heart of man seem to be drawn out, and we are become timorous, desponding whimperers."

It is the same wherever we open his books. He must spur on, feed up, bring forward the dormant character of his countrymen. When he goes to England, he sees in English life nothing except those elements which are deficient in American life. If you wish a catalogue of what America has not, read English Traits. Emerson's patriotism had the effect of expanding his philosophy. Today we know the value of physique, for science has taught it, but it was hardly discovered in his day, and his philosophy affords no basis for it. Emerson in this matter transcends his philosophy. When in England, he was fairly made drunk with the physical life he found there. He is like Caspar Hauser gazing for the first time on green fields. English Traits is the ruddiest book he ever wrote. It is a hymn to force, honesty, and physical well-being, and ends with the dominant note of his belief: "By this general activity and by this sacredness of individuals, they [the English] have in seven hundred years evolved the principles of freedom. It is the land of patriots, martyrs, sages, and bards, and if the ocean out of which it emerged should wash it away, it will be remembered as an island famous for immortal laws, for the announcements of original right which make the stone tables of liberty." He had found in England free speech, personal courage, and reverence for the individual.

No convulsion could shake Emerson or make his view unsteady even for an instant. What no one else saw, he saw, and he saw nothing else. Not a boy in the land welcomed the outbreak of the war so fiercely as did this shy village philosopher, then at the age of fifty-eight. He saw that war was the cure for cowardice, moral as well as physical. It was not the cause of the slave that moved him; it was not the cause of the Union for which he cared a farthing. It was something deeper than either of these things for which he had been battling all his life. It was the cause of character against convention. Whatever else the war might bring, it was sure to bring in character, to leave behind it a file of heroes; if not heroes, then villains, but in any case strong men. On the 9th of April, 1861, three days before Fort Sumter was bombarded, he had spoken with equanimity of "the downfall of our character-destroying civilization.... We find that civilization crowed too soon, that our triumphs were treacheries; we had opened the wrong door and let the enemy into the castle."

"Ah," he said, when the firing began, "sometimes gunpowder smells good." Soon after the attack on Sumter he said in a public address, "We have been very homeless for some years past, say since 1850; but now we have a country again.... The war was an eye-opener, and showed men of all parties and opinions the value of those primary forces that lie beneath all political action." And it was almost a personal pledge when he said at the Harvard Commemoration in 1865, "We shall not again disparage America, now that we have seen what men it will bear."

The place which Emerson forever occupies as a great critic is defined by the same sharp outlines that mark his work, in whatever light and from whatever side we approach it. A critic in the modern sense he was not, for his point of view is fixed, and he reviews the world like a search-light placed on the top of a tall tower. He lived too early and at too great a distance from the forum of European thought to absorb the ideas of evolution and give place to them in his philosophy. Evolution does not graft well upon the Platonic Idealism, nor are physiology and the kindred sciences sympathetic. Nothing aroused Emerson's indignation more than the attempts of the medical faculty and of phrenologists to classify, and therefore limit individuals. "The grossest ignorance does not disgust me like this ignorant knowingness."

We miss in Emerson the underlying conception of growth, of development, so characteristic of the thought of our own day, and which, for instance, is found everywhere latent in Browning's poetry. Browning regards character as the result of experience and as an ever changing growth. To Emerson, character is rather an entity complete and eternal from the beginning. He is probably the last great writer to look at life from a stationary standpoint. There is a certain lack of the historic sense in all he has written. The ethical assumption that all men are exactly alike permeates his work. In his mind, Socrates, Marco Polo, and General Jackson stand surrounded by the same atmosphere, or rather stand as mere naked characters surrounded by no atmosphere at all. He is probably the last great writer who will fling about classic anecdotes as if they were club gossip. In the discussion of morals, this assumption does little harm. The stories and proverbs which illustrate the thought of the moralist generally concern only those simple relations of life which are common to all ages. There is charm in this familiar dealing with antiquity. The classics are thus domesticated and made real to us. What matter if Aesop appears a little too much like an American citizen, so long as his points tell?

It is in Emerson's treatment of the fine arts that we begin to notice his want of historic sense. Art endeavors to express subtle and ever changing feelings by means of conventions which are as protean as the forms of a cloud; and the man who in speaking on the plastic arts makes the assumption that all men are alike will reveal before he has uttered three sentences that he does not know what art is, that he has never experienced any form of sensation from it. Emerson lived in a time and clime where there was no plastic art, and he was obliged to arrive at his ideas about art by means of a highly complex process of reasoning. He dwelt constantly in a spiritual place which was the very focus of high moral fervor. This was his enthusiasm, this was his revelation, and from it he reasoned out the probable meaning of the fine arts. "This," thought Emerson, his eye rolling in a fine frenzy of moral feeling, "this must be what Apelles experienced, this fervor is the passion of Bramante. I understand the Parthenon." And so he projected his feelings about morality into the field of the plastic arts. He deals very freely and rather indiscriminately with the names of artists,—Phidias, Raphael,

Salvator Rosa,—and he speaks always in such a way that it is impossible to connect what he says with any impression we have ever received from the works of those masters.

In fact, Emerson has never in his life felt the normal appeal of any painting, or any sculpture, or any architecture, or any music. These things, of which he does not know the meaning in real life, he yet uses, and uses constantly, as symbols to convey ethical truths. The result is that his books are full of blind places, like the notes which will not strike on a sick piano.

It is interesting to find that the one art of which Emerson did have a direct understanding, the art of poetry, gave him some insight into the relation of the artist to his vehicle. In his essay on Shakespeare there is a full recognition of the debt of Shakespeare to his times. This essay is filled with the historic sense. We ought not to accuse Emerson because he lacked appreciation of the fine arts, but rather admire the truly Goethean spirit in which he insisted upon the reality of arts of which he had no understanding. This is the same spirit which led him to insist on the value of the Eastern poets. Perhaps there exist a few scholars who can tell us how far Emerson understood or misunderstood Saadi and Firdusi and the Koran. But we need not be disturbed for his learning. It is enough that he makes us recognize that these men were men too, and that their writings mean something not unknowable to us. The East added nothing to Emerson, but gave him a few trappings of speech. The whole of his mysticism is to be found in Nature, written before he knew the sages of the Orient, and it is not improbable that there is some real connection between his own mysticism and the mysticism of the Eastern poets.

Emerson's criticism on men and books is like the test of a great chemist who seeks one or two elements. He burns a bit of the stuff in his incandescent light, shows the lines of it in his spectrum, and there an end.

It was a thought of genius that led him to write Representative Men. The scheme of this book gave play to every illumination of his mind, and it pinned him down to the objective, to the field of vision under his microscope. The table of contents of Representative Men is the dial of his education. It is as follows: Uses of Great Men; Plato, or The Philosopher; Plato, New Readings; Swedenborg, or The Mystic; Montaigne, or The Sceptic; Shakespeare, or The Poet; Napoleon, or The Man of the World; Goethe, or The Writer. The predominance of the writers over all other types of men is not cited to show Emerson's interest in The Writer, for we know his interest centred in the practical man,—even his ideal scholar is a practical man,—but to show the sources of his illustration. Emerson's library was the old-fashioned gentleman's library. His mines of thought were the world's classics. This is one reason why he so quickly gained an international currency. His very subjects in Representative Men are of universal interest, and he is limited only by certain inevitable local conditions. Representative Men is thought by many persons to be his best book. It is certainly filled with the strokes of a master. There exists no more profound criticism than Emerson's analysis of Goethe and of Napoleon, by both of whom he was at once fascinated and repelled.

II

The attitude of Emerson's mind toward reformers results so logically from his philosophy that it is easily understood. He saw in them people who sought something as a panacea or as an end in itself. To speak strictly and not irreverently, he had his own panacea,—the development of each individual; and he was impatient of any other. He did not believe in association. The very idea of it involved a surrender by the individual of some portion of his identity, and of course all the reformers worked through their associations. With their general aims he sympathized. "These reforms," he wrote, "are our contemporaries; they are ourselves, our own light and sight and conscience; they only name the relation which subsists between us and the vicious institutions which they go to rectify." But with the methods of the reformers he had no sympathy: "He who aims at progress should aim at an infinite, not at a special benefit. The reforms whose fame now fills the land with temperance, anti-slavery, non-resistance, no-government, equal labor, fair and generous as each appears, are poor bitter things when prosecuted for themselves as an end." Again: "The young men who have been vexing society for these last years with regenerative methods seem to have made this mistake: they all exaggerated some special means, and all failed to see that the reform of reforms must be accomplished without means."

Emerson did not at first discriminate between the movement of the Abolitionists and the hundred and one other reform movements of the period; and in this lack of discrimination lies a point of extraordinary interest. The Abolitionists, as it afterwards turned out, had in fact got hold of the issue which was to control the fortunes of the republic for thirty years. The difference between them and the other reformers was this: that the Abolitionists were men set in motion by the primary and unreasoning passion of pity. Theory played small part in the movement. It grew by the excitement which exhibitions of cruelty will arouse in the minds of sensitive people.

It is not to be denied that the social conditions in Boston in 1831 foreboded an outbreak in some form. If the abolition excitement had not drafted off the rising forces, there might have been a Merry Mount, an epidemic of crime or insanity, or a mob of some sort. The abolition movement afforded the purest form of an indulgence in human feeling that was ever offered to men. It was intoxicating. It made the agitators perfectly happy. They sang at their work and bubbled over with exhilaration. They were the only people in the United States, at this time, who were enjoying an exalted, glorifying, practical activity.

But Emerson at first lacked the touchstone, whether of intellect or of heart, to see the difference between this particular movement and the other movements then in progress. Indeed, in so far as he sees any difference between the Abolitionists and the rest, it is that the Abolitionists were more objectionable and distasteful to him. "Those," he said, "who are urging with most ardor what are called the greatest benefits to mankind are narrow, conceited, self-pleasing men, and affect us as the insane do." And again: "By the side of these men [the idealists] the hot agitators have a certain cheap and ridiculous air; they even look smaller than others. Of the two, I own I like the speculators the best. They have some piety which looks with faith to a fair future unprofaned by rash and unequal attempts to realize it." He was drawn into the abolition cause by having the truth brought home to him that these people were fighting for the Moral Law. He was slow in seeing this, because in their methods they represented everything he most condemned. As soon, however, as he was convinced, he was ready to lecture for them and to give them the weight of his approval. In 1844 he was already practically an Abolitionist, and his feelings upon the matter deepened steadily in intensity ever after.

The most interesting page of Emerson's published journal is the following, written at some time previous to 1844; the exact date is not given. A like page, whether written or unwritten, may be read into the private annals of every man who lived before the war. Emerson has, with unconscious mastery, photographed the half-spectre that stalked in the minds of all. He wrote: "I had occasion to say the other day to Elizabeth Hoar that I like best the strong and worthy persons, like her father, who support the social order without hesitation or misgiving. I like these; they never incommode us by exciting grief, pity, or perturbation of any sort. But the professed philanthropists, it is strange and horrible to say, are an altogether odious set of people, whom one would shun as the worst of bores and canters. But my conscience, my unhappy conscience respects that hapless class who see the faults and stains of our social order, and who pray and strive incessantly to right the wrong; this annoying class of men and women, though they commonly find the work altogether beyond their faculty, and their results are, for the present, distressing. They are partial, and apt to magnify their own. Yes, and the prostrate penitent, also,—he is not comprehensive, he is not philosophical in those tears and groans. Yet I feel that under him and his partiality and exclusiveness is the earth and the sea and all that in them is, and the axis around which the universe revolves passes through his body where he stands."

It was the defection of Daniel Webster that completed the conversion of Emerson and turned him from an adherent into a propagandist of abolition. Not pity for the slave, but indignation at the violation of the Moral Law by Daniel Webster, was at the bottom of Emerson's anger. His abolitionism was secondary to his main mission, his main enthusiasm. It is for this reason that he stands on a plane of intellect where he might, under other circumstances, have met and defeated Webster. After the 7th of March, 1850, he recognized in Webster the embodiment of all that he hated. In his attacks on Webster, Emerson trembles to his inmost fibre with antagonism. He is savage, destructive, personal, bent on death.

This exhibition of Emerson as a fighting animal is magnificent, and explains his life. There is no other instance of his ferocity. No other nature but Webster's ever so moved him; but it was time to be moved, and Webster was a man of his size. Had these two great men of New England been matched in training as they were matched in endowment, and had they then faced each other in debate, they would not have been found to differ so greatly in power. Their natures were electrically repellent, but from which did the greater force radiate? Their education differed so radically that it is impossible to compare them, but if you translate the Phi Beta Kappa address into politics, you have something stronger than Webster,—something that recalls Chatham; and Emerson would have had this advantage,—that he was not afraid. As it was, he left his library and took the stump. Mr. Cabot has given us extracts from his speeches:—

"The tameness is indeed complete; all are involved in one hot haste of terror,—presidents of colleges and professors, saints and brokers, lawyers and manufacturers; not a liberal recollection, not so much as a snatch of an old song for freedom, dares intrude on their passive obedience.... Mr. Webster, perhaps, is only following the laws of his blood and constitution. I suppose his pledges were not quite natural to him. He is a man who lives by his memory; a man of the past, not a man of faith and of hope. All the drops of his blood have eyes that look downward, and his finely developed understanding only works truly and with all its force when it stands for animal good; that is, for property. He looks at the Union as an estate, a large farm, and is excellent in the completeness of his defence of it so far. What he finds already written he will defend. Lucky that so much had got well written when he came, for he has no faith in the power of self-government. Not the smallest municipal provision, if it were new, would receive his sanction. In Massachusetts, in 1776, he would, beyond all question, have been a refugee. He praises Adams and Jefferson, but it is a past Adams and Jefferson. A present Adams or Jefferson he would denounce. . . . But one thing appears certain to me: that the Union is at an end as soon as an immoral law is enacted. He who writes a crime into the statute book digs under the foundations of the Capitol. . . . The words of John Randolph, wiser than he knew, have been ringing ominously in all echoes for thirty years: 'We do not govern the people of the North by our black slaves, but by their own white slaves.' . . . They come down now like the cry of fate, in the moment when they are fulfilled."

The exasperation of Emerson did not subside, but went on increasing during the next four years, and on March 7, 1854, he read his lecture on the Fugitive Slave Law at the New York Tabernacle: "I have lived all my life without suffering any inconvenience from American Slavery. I never saw it; I never heard the whip; I never felt the check on my free speech and action, until the other day, when Mr. Webster, by his personal influence, brought the Fugitive Slave Law on the country. I say Mr. Webster, for though the bill was not his, it is yet notorious that he was the life and soul of it, that he gave it all he had. It cost him his life, and under the shadow of his great name inferior men sheltered themselves, threw their ballots for it, and made the law. . . . Nobody doubts that Daniel Webster could make a good speech. Nobody doubts that there were good and plausible things to be said on the part of the South. But this is not a question of ingenuity, not a question of syllogisms, but of sides. *How came he there?* . . . But the question which history will ask is broader. In the final hour when he was forced by the peremptory necessity of the closing armies to take a side,—did he take the part of great principles, the side of humanity and justice, or the side of abuse, and oppression and chaos? . . . He did as immoral men usually do,—made very low bows to the Christian Church and went through all the Sunday decorums, but when allusion was made to the question of duty and the sanctions of morality, he very frankly said, at Albany, 'Some higher law, something existing somewhere between here and the heaven—I do not know where.' And if the reporters say true, this wretched atheism found some laughter in the company."

It was too late for Emerson to shine as a political debater. On May 14, 1857, Longfellow wrote in his diary, "It is rather painful to see Emerson in the arena of politics, hissed and hooted at by young law students." Emerson records a similar experience at a later date: "If I were dumb, yet would I have gone and mowed and muttered or made signs. The mob roared whenever I attempted to speak, and after several beginnings I withdrew." There is nothing "painful" here: it is the sublime exhibition of a great soul in bondage to circumstance.

The thing to be noted is that this is the same man, in the same state of excitement about the same idea, who years before spoke out in The American Scholar, in the Essays, and in the Lectures.

What was it that had aroused in Emerson such Promethean antagonism in 1837 but those same forces which in 1850 came to their culmination and assumed visible shape in the person of Daniel Webster? The formal victory of Webster drew Emerson into the arena, and made a dramatic episode in his life. But his battle with those forces had begun thirteen years earlier, when he threw down the gauntlet to them in his Phi Beta Kappa oration. Emerson by his writings did more than any other man to rescue the youth of the next generation and fit them for the fierce times to follow. It will not be denied that he sent ten thousand sons to the war.

In speaking of Emerson's attitude toward the anti-slavery cause, it has been possible to dispense with any survey of that movement, because the movement was simple and specific and is well remembered. But when we come to analyze the relations he bore to some of the local agitations of his day, it becomes necessary to weave in with the matter a discussion of certain tendencies deeply imbedded in the life of his times, and of which he himself was in a sense an outcome. In speaking of the Transcendentalists, who were essentially the children of the Puritans, we must begin with some study of the chief traits of Puritanism.

What parts the factors of climate, circumstance, and religion have respectively played in the development of the New England character no analysis can determine. We may trace the imaginary influence of a harsh creed in the lines of the face. We may sometimes follow from generation to generation the course of a truth which at first sustained the spirit of man, till we see it petrify into a dogma which now kills the spirits of men. Conscience may destroy the character. The tragedy of the New England judge enforcing the Fugitive Slave Law was no new spectacle in New England. A dogmatic crucifixion of the natural instincts had been in progress there for two hundred years. Emerson, who is more free from dogma than any other teacher that can be named, yet comes very near being dogmatic in his reiteration of the Moral Law.

Whatever volume of Emerson we take up, the Moral Law holds the same place in his thoughts. It is the one statable revelation of truth which he is ready to stake his all upon. "The illusion that strikes me as the masterpiece in that ring of illusions which our life is, is the timidity with which we assert our moral sentiment. We are made of it, the world is built by it, things endure as they share it; all beauty, all health, all intelligence exist by it; yet we shrink to speak of it or range ourselves by its side. Nay, we presume strength of him or them who deny it. Cities go against it, the college goes against it, the courts snatch any precedent at any vicious form of law to rule it out; legislatures listen with appetite to declamations against it and vote it down."

With this very beautiful and striking passage no one will quarrel, nor will any one misunderstand it.

The following passage has the same sort of poetical truth. "Things are saturated with the moral law. There is no escape from it. Violets and grass preach it; rain and snow, wind and tides, every change, every cause in Nature is nothing but a disguised missionary." . . .

But Emerson is not satisfied with metaphor. "We affirm that in all men is this majestic perception and command; that it is the presence of the eternal in each perishing man; that it distances and degrades all statements of whatever saints, heroes, poets, as obscure and confused stammerings before its silent revelation. *They* report the truth. *It is the truth.*" In this last extract we have Emerson actually affirming that his dogma of the Moral Law is Absolute Truth. He thinks it not merely a form of truth, like the old theologies, but very distinguishable from all other forms in the past.

Curiously enough, his statement of the law grows dogmatic and incisive in proportion as he approaches the borderland between his law and the natural instincts: "The last revelation of intellect and of sentiment is that in a manner it severs the man from all other men; makes known to him *that the spiritual powers are sufficient to him if no other being existed;* that he is to deal absolutely in the world, as if he alone were a system and a state, and though all should perish could make all anew." Here we have the dogma applied, and we see in it only a new form of old Calvinism as cruel as Calvinism, and not much different from its original. The italics are not Emerson's, but are inserted to bring out an idea which is everywhere prevalent in his teaching.

In this final form, the Moral Law, by insisting that sheer conscience can slake the thirst that rises in the soul, is convicted of falsehood; and this heartless falsehood is the same falsehood that has been put into the porridge of every Puritan child for six generations. A grown man can digest doctrine and sleep at night. But a young person of high purpose and strong will, who takes such a lie as this half-truth and feeds on it as on the bread of life, will suffer. It will injure the action of his heart. Truly the fathers have eaten sour grapes, therefore the children's teeth are set on edge.

⁂

To understand the civilization of cities, we must look at the rural population from which they draw their life. We have recently had our attention called to the last remnants of that village life so reverently gathered up by Miss Wilkins, and of which Miss Emily Dickinson was the last authentic voice. The spirit of this age has examined with an almost pathological interest this rescued society. We must go to it if we would understand Emerson, who is the blossoming of its culture. We must study it if we would arrive at any intelligent and general view of that miscellaneous crop of individuals who have been called the Transcendentalists.

Between 1830 and 1840 there were already signs in New England that the nutritive and reproductive forces of society were not quite wholesome, not exactly well adjusted. Self-repression was the religion which had been inherited. "Distrust Nature" was the motto written upon the front of the temple. What would have happened to that society if left to itself for another hundred years no man can guess. It was rescued by the two great regenerators of mankind, new land and war. The dispersion came, as Emerson said of the barbarian conquests of Rome, not a day too soon. It happened that the country at large stood in need of New England as much as New England stood in need of the country. This congested virtue, in order to be saved, must be scattered. This ferment, in order to be kept wholesome, must be used as leaven to leaven the whole lump. "As you know," says Emerson in his Eulogy on Boston, "New England supplies annually a large detachment of preachers and schoolmasters and private tutors to the interior of the South and West.... We are willing to see our sons emigrate, as to see our hives swarm. That is what they were made to do, and what the land wants and invites."

For purposes of yeast, there was never such leaven as the Puritan stock. How little the natural force of the race had really abated became apparent when it was placed under healthy conditions, given land to till, foes to fight, the chance to renew its youth like the eagle. But during this period the relief had not yet come. The terrible pressure of Puritanism and conservatism in New England was causing a revolt not only of the Abolitionists, but of another class of people of a type not so virile as they. The times have been smartly described by Lowell in his essay on Thoreau:—

"Every possible form of intellectual and physical dyspepsia brought forth its gospel. Bran had its prophets.... Everybody had a Mission (with a capital M) to attend to everybody else's business. No brain but had its private maggot, which must have found pitiably short commons sometimes. Not a few impecunious zealots abjured the use of money (unless earned by other people), professing to live on the internal revenues of the spirit. Some had an assurance of instant millennium so soon as hooks and eyes should be substituted for buttons. Communities were established where everything was to be common but common sense.... Conventions were held for every hitherto inconceivable purpose."

Whatever may be said of the Transcendentalists, it must not be forgotten that they represented an elevation of feeling, which through them qualified the next generation, and can be traced in the life of New England to-day. The strong intrinsic character lodged in these recusants was later made manifest; for many of them became the best citizens of the commonwealth,—statesmen, merchants, soldiers, men and women of affairs. They retained their idealism while becoming practical men. There is hardly an example of what we should have thought would be common in their later lives, namely, a reaction from so much ideal effort, and a plunge into cynicism and malice, scoundrelism and the flesh-pots. In their early life they resembled the Abolitionists in their devotion to an idea; but with the Transcendentalists self-culture and the aesthetic and sentimental education took the place of more public aims. They seem also to have been persons of greater social refinement than the Abolitionists.

The Transcendentalists were sure of only one thing,—that society as constituted was all wrong. In this their main belief they were right. They were men and women whose fundamental need was activity, contact with real life, and the opportunity for social expansion; and they keenly felt the chill and fictitious character of the reigning conventionalities. The rigidity of behavior which at this time characterized the Bostonians seemed sometimes ludicrous and sometimes disagreeable to the foreign visitor. There was great gravity, together with a certain pomp and dumbness, and these things were supposed to be natural to the inhabitants and to give them joy. People are apt to forget that such masks are never worn with ease. They result from the application of an inflexible will, and always inflict discomfort. The Transcendentalists found themselves all but stifled in a society as artificial in its decorum as the court of France during the last years of Louis XIV.

Emerson was in no way responsible for the movement, although he got the credit of having evoked it by his teaching. He was elder brother to it, and was generated by its parental forces; but even if Emerson had never lived, the Transcendentalists would have appeared. He was their victim rather than their cause. He was always tolerant of them and sometimes amused at them, and disposed to treat them lightly. It is impossible to analyze their case with more astuteness than he did in an editorial letter in The Dial. The letter is cold, but is a masterpiece of good sense. He had, he says, received fifteen letters on the Prospects of Culture. "Excellent reasons have been shown us why the writers, obviously persons of sincerity and elegance, should be dissatisfied with the life they lead, and with their company.... They want a friend to whom they can speak and from whom they may hear now and then a reasonable word." After discussing one or two of their proposals,—one of which was that the tiresome "uncles and aunts" of the enthusiasts should be placed by themselves in one delightful village, the dough, as Emerson says, be placed in one pan and the leaven in another,—he continues: "But it would be unjust not to remind our younger friends that whilst this aspiration has always made its mark in the lives of men of thought, in vigorous individuals it does not remain a detached object, but is satisfied along with the satisfaction of other aims." Young Americans "are educated above the work of their times and country, and disdain it. Many of the more acute minds pass into a lofty criticism . . . which only embitters their sensibility to the evil, and widens the feeling of hostility between them and the citizens at large. . . . We should not know where to find in literature any record of so much unbalanced intellectuality, such undeniable apprehension without talent, so much power without equal applicability, as our young men pretend to. . . . The balance of mind and body will redress itself fast enough. Superficialness is the real distemper. . . . It is certain that speculation is no succedaneum for life." He then turns to find the cure for these distempers in the farm lands of Illinois, at that time already being fenced in "almost like New England itself," and closes with a suggestion that so long as there is a woodpile in the yard, and the "wrongs of the Indian, of the Negro, of the emigrant, remain unmitigated," relief might be found even nearer home.

In his lecture on the Transcendentalists he says: ". . . But their solitary and fastidious manners not only withdraw them from the conversation, but from the labors of the world: they are not good citizens, not good members of society; unwillingly they bear their part of the public and private burdens; they do not willingly share in the public charities, in the public religious rites, in the enterprises of education, of missions foreign and domestic, in the abolition of the slave-trade, or in the temperance society. They do not even like to vote." A less sympathetic observer, Harriet Martineau, wrote of them: "While Margaret Fuller and her adult pupils sat 'gorgeously dressed,' talking about Mars and Venus, Plato and Goethe, and fancying themselves the elect of the earth in intellect and refinement, the liberties of the republic were running out as fast as they could go at a breach which another sort of elect persons were devoting themselves to repair; and my complaint against the 'gorgeous' pedants was that they regarded their preservers as hewers of wood and drawers of water, and their work as a less vital one than the pedantic orations which were spoiling a set of well-meaning women in a pitiable way." Harriet Martineau, whose whole work was practical, and who wrote her journal in 1855 and in the light of history, was hardly able to do justice to these unpractical but sincere spirits.

Emerson was divided from the Transcendentalists by his common sense. His shrewd business intellect made short work of their schemes. Each one of their social projects contained some covert economic weakness, which always turned out to lie in an attack upon the integrity of the individual, and which Emerson of all men could be counted on to detect. He was divided from them also by the fact that he was a man of genius, who had sought out and fought out his means of expression. He was a great artist, and as such he was a complete being. No one could give to him nor take from him. His yearnings found fruition in expression. He was sure of his place and of his use in this world. But the Transcendentalists were neither geniuses nor artists nor complete beings. Nor had they found their places or uses as yet. They were men and women seeking light. They walked in dry places, seeking rest and finding none. The Transcendentalists are not collectively important because their *Sturm und Drang* was intellectual and bloodless. Though Emerson admonish and Harriet Martineau condemn, yet from the memorials that survive, one is more impressed with the sufferings than with the ludicrousness of these persons. There is something distressing about their letters, their talk, their memoirs, their interminable diaries. They worry and contort and introspect. They rave and dream. They peep and theorize. They cut open the bellows of life to see where the wind comes from. Margaret Fuller analyzes Emerson, and Emerson Margaret Fuller. It is not a wholesome ebullition of vitality. It is a nightmare, in which the emotions, the terror, the agony, the rapture, are all unreal, and have no vital content, no consequence in the world outside. It is positively wonderful that so much excitement and so much suffering should have left behind nothing in the field of art which is valuable. All that intelligence could do toward solving problems for his friends Emerson did. But there are situations in life in which the intelligence is helpless, and in which something else, something perhaps possessed by a ploughboy, is more divine than Plato.

If it were not pathetic, there would be something cruel—indeed there is something cruel—in Emerson's incapacity to deal with Margaret Fuller. He wrote to her on October 24, 1840: "My dear Margaret, I have your frank and noble and affecting letter, and yet I think I could wish it unwritten. I ought never to have suffered you to lead me into any conversation or writing on our relation, a topic from which with all persons my Genius warns me away."

The letter proceeds with unimpeachable emptiness and integrity in the same strain. In 1841 he writes in his diary: "Strange, cold-warm, attractive-repelling conversation with Margaret, whom I always admire, most revere when I nearest see, and sometimes love; yet whom I freeze and who freezes me to silence when we promise to come nearest."

Human sentiment was known to Emerson mainly in the form of pain. His nature shunned it; he cast it off as quickly as possible. There is a word or two in the essay on Love which seems to show that the inner and diaphanous core of this seraph had once, but not for long, been shot with blood: he recalls only the pain of it. His relations with Margaret Fuller seem never normal, though they lasted for years. This brilliant woman was in distress. She was asking for bread, and he was giving her a stone, and neither of them was conscious of what was passing. This is pitiful. It makes us clutch about us to catch hold, if we somehow may, of the hand of a man.

There was manliness in Horace Greeley, under whom Miss Fuller worked on the New York Tribune not many years afterward. She wrote: "Mr. Greeley I like,—nay, more, love. He is in his habit a plebeian, in his heart a nobleman. His abilities in his own way are great. He believes in mine to a surprising degree. We are true friends."

This anaemic incompleteness of Emerson's character can be traced to the philosophy of his race; at least it can be followed in that philosophy. There is an implication of a fundamental falsehood in every bit of Transcendentalism, including Emerson. That falsehood consists in the theory of the self-sufficiency of each individual, men and women alike. Margaret Fuller is a good example of the effect of this philosophy, because her history afterward showed that she was constituted like other human beings, was dependent upon human relationship, and was not only a very noble, but also a very womanly creature. Her marriage, her Italian life, and her tragic death light up with the splendor of reality the earlier and unhappy period of her life. This woman had been driven into her vagaries by the lack of something which she did not know existed, and which she sought blindly in metaphysics. Harriet Martineau writes of her: "It is the most grievous loss I have almost ever known in private history, the deferring of Margaret Fuller's married life so long. That noble last period of her life is happily on record as well as the earlier." The hardy Englishwoman has here laid a kind human hand on the weakness of New England, and seems to be unconscious that she is making a revelation as to the whole Transcendental movement. But the point is this: there was no one within reach of Margaret Fuller, in her early days, who knew what was her need. One offered her Kant, one Comte, one Fourier, one Swedenborg, one the Moral Law. You cannot feed the heart on these things.

Yet there is a bright side to this New England spirit, which seems, if we look only to the graver emotions, so dry, dismal, and deficient. A bright and cheery courage appears in certain natures of which the sun has made conquest, that almost reconciles us to all loss, so splendid is the outcome. The practical, dominant, insuppressible active temperaments who have a word for every emergency, and who carry the controlled force of ten men at their disposal, are the fruits of this same spirit. Emerson knew not tears, but he and the hundred other beaming and competent characters which New England has produced make us almost envy their state. They give us again the old Stoics at their best.

Very closely connected with this subject—the crisp and cheery New England temperament—lies another which any discussion of Emerson must bring up,—namely, Asceticism. It is probable that in dealing with Emerson's feelings about the plastic arts we have to do with what is really the inside, or metaphysical side, of the same phenomena which present themselves on the outside, or physical side, in the shape of asceticism.

Emerson's natural asceticism is revealed to us in almost every form in which history can record a man. It is in his philosophy, in his style, in his conduct, and in his appearance. It was, however, not in his voice. Mr. Cabot, with that reverence for which every one must feel personally grateful to him, has preserved a description of Emerson by the New York journalist, N.P. Willis: "It is a voice with shoulders in it, which he has not; with lungs in it far larger than his; with a walk which the public never see; with a fist in it which his own hand never gave him the model for; and with a gentleman in it which his parochial and 'bare-necessaries-of-life' sort of exterior gives no other betrayal of. We can imagine nothing in nature (which seems too to have a type for everything) like the want of correspondence between the Emerson that goes in at the eye and the Emerson that goes in at the ear. A heavy and vase-like blossom of a magnolia, with fragrance enough to perfume a whole wilderness, which should be lifted by a whirlwind and dropped into a branch of aspen, would not seem more as if it could never have grown there than Emerson's voice seems inspired and foreign to his visible and natural body." Emerson's ever exquisite and wonderful good taste seems closely connected with this asceticism, and it is probable that his taste influenced his views and conduct to some small extent.

The anti-slavery people were not always refined. They were constantly doing things which were tactically very effective, but were not calculated to attract the over-sensitive. Garrison's rampant and impersonal egotism was good politics, but bad taste. Wendell Phillips did not hesitate upon occasion to deal in personalities of an exasperating kind. One sees a certain shrinking in Emerson from the taste of the Abolitionists. It was not merely their doctrines or their methods which offended him. He at one time refused to give Wendell Phillips his hand because of Phillips's treatment of his friend, Judge Hoar. One hardly knows whether to be pleased at Emerson for showing a human weakness, or annoyed at him for not being more of a man. The anecdote is valuable in both lights. It is like a tiny speck on the crystal of his character which shows us the exact location of the orb, and it is the best illustration of the feeling of the times which has come down to us.

If by "asceticism" we mean an experiment in starving the senses, there is little harm in it. Nature will soon reassert her dominion, and very likely our perceptions will be sharpened by the trial. But "natural asceticism" is a thing hardly to be distinguished from functional weakness. What is natural asceticism but a lack of vigor? Does it not tend to close the avenues between the soul and the universe? "Is it not so much death?" The accounts of Emerson show him to have been a man in whom there was almost a hiatus between the senses and the most inward spirit of life. The lower register of sensations and emotions which domesticate a man into fellowship with common life was weak. Genial familiarity was to him impossible; laughter was almost a pain. "It is not the sea and poverty and pursuit that separate us. Here is Alcott by my door,—yet is the union more profound? No! the sea, vocation, poverty, are seeming fences, but man is insular and cannot be touched. Every man is an infinitely repellent orb, and holds his individual being on that condition. . . . Most of the persons whom I see in my own house I see across a gulf; I cannot go to them nor they come to me."

This aloofness of Emerson must be remembered only as blended with his benignity. "His friends were all that knew him," and, as Dr. Holmes said, "his smile was the well-remembered line of Terence written out in living features." Emerson's journals show the difficulty of his intercourse even with himself. He could not reach himself at will, nor could another reach him. The sensuous and ready contact with nature which more carnal people enjoy was unknown to him. He had eyes for the New England landscape, but for no other scenery. If there is one supreme sensation reserved for man, it is the vision of Venice seen from the water. This sight greeted Emerson at the age of thirty. The famous city, as he approached it by boat, "looked for some time like nothing but New York. It is a great oddity, a city for beavers, but to my thought a most disagreeable residence. You feel always in prison and solitary. It is as if you were always at sea. I soon had enough of it."

Emerson's contempt for travel and for the "rococo toy," Italy, is too well known to need citation. It proceeds from the same deficiency of sensation. His eyes saw nothing; his ears heard nothing. He believed that men travelled for distraction and to kill time. The most vulgar plutocrat could not be blinder to beauty nor bring home less from Athens than this cultivated saint. Everything in the world which must be felt with a glow in the breast, in order to be understood, was to him dead-letter. Art was a name to him; music was a name to him; love was a name to him. His essay on Love is a nice compilation of compliments and elegant phrases ending up with some icy morality. It seems very well fitted for a gift-book or an old-fashioned lady's annual.

"The lovers delight in endearments, in avowals of love, in comparisons of their regards.... The soul which is in the soul of each, craving a perfect beatitude, detects incongruities, defects, and disproportion in the behavior of the other. Hence arise surprise, expostulation, and pain. Yet that which drew them to each other was signs of loveliness, signs of virtue; and these virtues are there, however eclipsed. They appear and reappear and continue to attract; but the regard changes, quits the sign and attaches to the substance. This repairs the wounded affection. Meantime, as life wears on, it proves a game of permutation and combination of all possible positions of the parties, to employ all the resources of each, and acquaint each with the weakness of the other. . . . At last they discover that all which at first drew them together—those once sacred features, that magical play of charms—was deciduous, had a prospective end like the scaffolding by which the house was built, and the purification of the intellect and the heart from year to year is the real marriage, foreseen and prepared from the first, and wholly above their consciousness. . . . Thus are we put in training for a love which knows not sex nor person nor partiality, but which seeks wisdom and virtue everywhere, to the end of increasing virtue and wisdom. . . . There are moments when the affections rule and absorb the man, and make his happiness dependent on a person or persons. But in health the mind is presently seen again," etc.

All this is not love, but the merest literary coquetry. Love is different from this. Lady Burton, when a very young girl, and six years before her engagement, met Burton at Boulogne. They met in the street, but did not speak. A few days later they were formally introduced at a dance. Of this she writes: "That was a night of nights. He waltzed with me once, and spoke to me several times. I kept the sash where he put his arm around me and my gloves, and never wore them again."

A glance at what Emerson says about marriage shows that he suspected that institution. He can hardly speak of it without some sort of caveat or precaution. "Though the stuff of tragedy and of romances is in a moral union of two superior persons whose confidence in each other for long years, out of sight and in sight, and against all appearances, is at last justified by victorious proof of probity to gods and men, causing joyful emotions, tears, and glory,—though there be for heroes this *moral union*, yet they too are as far as ever from an intellectual union, and the moral is for low and external purposes, like the corporation of a ship's company or of a fire club." In speaking of modern novels, he says: "There is no new element, no power, no furtherance. 'T is only confectionery, not the raising of new corn. Great is the poverty of their inventions. *She was beautiful, and he fell in love.* . . . Happy will that house be in which the relations are formed by character; after the highest and not after the lowest; the house in which character marries and not confusion and a miscellany of unavowable motives.... To each occurs soon after puberty, some event, or society or way of living, which becomes the crisis of life and the chief fact in their history. In women it is love and marriage (which is more reasonable), and yet it is pitiful to date and measure all the facts and sequel of an unfolding life from such a youthful and generally inconsiderate period as the age of courtship and marriage.... Women more than all are the element and kingdom of illusion. Being fascinated they fascinate. They see through Claude Lorraines. And how dare any one, if he could, pluck away the coulisses, stage effects and ceremonies by which they live? Too pathetic, too pitiable, is the region of affection, and its atmosphere always liable to mirage."

We are all so concerned that a man who writes about love shall tell the truth that if he chance to start from premises which are false or mistaken, his conclusions will appear not merely false, but offensive. It makes no matter how exalted the personal character of the writer may be. Neither sanctity nor intellect nor moral enthusiasm, though they be intensified to the point of incandescence, can make up for a want of nature.

This perpetual splitting up of love into two species, one of which is condemned, but admitted to be useful—is it not degrading? There is in Emerson's theory of the relation between the sexes neither good sense, nor manly feeling, nor sound psychology. It is founded on none of these things. It is a pure piece of dogmatism, and reminds us that he was bred to the priesthood. We are not to imagine that there was in this doctrine anything peculiar to Emerson. But we are surprised to find the pessimism inherent in the doctrine overcome Emerson, to whom pessimism is foreign. Both doctrine and pessimism are a part of the Puritanism of the times. They show a society in which the intellect had long been used to analyze the affections, in which the head had become dislocated from the body. To this disintegration of the simple passion of love may be traced the lack of maternal tenderness characteristic of the New England nature. The relation between the blood and the brain was not quite normal in this civilization, nor in Emerson, who is its most remarkable representative.

If we take two steps backward from the canvas of this mortal life and glance at it impartially, we shall see that these matters of love and marriage pass like a pivot through the lives of almost every individual, and are, sociologically speaking, the *primum mobile* of the world. The books of any philosopher who slurs them or distorts them will hold up a false mirror to life. If an inhabitant of another planet should visit the earth, he would receive, on the whole, a truer notion of human life by attending an Italian opera than he would by reading Emerson's volumes. He would learn from the Italian opera that there were two sexes; and this, after all, is probably the fact with which the education of such a stranger ought to begin.

In a review of Emerson's personal character and opinions, we are thus led to see that his philosophy, which finds no room for the emotions, is a faithful exponent of his own and of the New England temperament, which distrusts and dreads the emotions. Regarded as a sole guide to life for a young person of strong conscience and undeveloped affections, his works might conceivably be even harmful because of their unexampled power of purely intellectual stimulation.

∾

Emerson's poetry has given rise to much heart-burning and disagreement. Some people do not like it. They fail to find the fire in the ice. On the other hand, his poems appeal not only to a large number of professed lovers of poetry, but also to a class of readers who find in Emerson an element for which they search the rest of poesy in vain.

It is the irony of fate that his admirers should be more than usually sensitive about his fame. This prophet who desired not to have followers, lest he too should become a cult and a convention, and whose main thesis throughout life was that piety is a crime, has been calmly canonized and embalmed in amber by the very forces he braved. He is become a tradition and a sacred relic. You must speak of him under your breath, and you may not laugh near his shrine.

Emerson's passion for nature was not like the passion of Keats or of Burns, of Coleridge or of Robert Browning; compared with these men he is cold. His temperature is below blood-heat, and his volume of poems stands on the shelf of English poets like the icy fish which in Caliban upon Setebos is described as finding himself thrust into the warm ooze of an ocean not his own.

But Emerson is a poet, nevertheless, a very extraordinary and rare man of genius, whose verses carry a world of their own within them. They are overshadowed by the greatness of his prose, but they are authentic. He is the chief poet of that school of which Emily Dickinson is a minor poet. His poetry is a successful spiritual deliverance of great interest. His worship of the New England landscape amounts to a religion. His poems do that most wonderful thing, make us feel that we are alone in the fields and with the trees,—not English fields nor French lanes, but New England meadows and uplands. There is no human creature in sight, not even Emerson is there, but the wind and the flowers, the wild birds, the fences, the transparent atmosphere, the breath of nature. There is a deep and true relation between the intellectual and almost dry brilliancy of Emerson's feelings and the landscape itself. Here is no defective English poet, no Shelley without the charm, but an American poet, a New England poet with two hundred years of New England culture and New England landscape in him.

People are forever speculating upon what will last, what posterity will approve, and some people believe that Emerson's poetry will outlive his prose. The question is idle. The poems are alive now, and they may or may not survive the race whose spirit they embody; but one thing is plain: they have qualities which have preserved poetry in the past. They are utterly indigenous and sincere. They are short. They represent a civilization and a climate.

His verse divides itself into several classes. We have the single lyrics, written somewhat in the style of the later seventeenth century. Of these The Humble Bee is the most exquisite, and although its tone and imagery can be traced to various well-known and dainty bits of poetry, it is by no means an imitation, but a masterpiece of fine taste. The Rhodora and Terminus and perhaps a few others belong to that class of poetry which, like Abou Ben Adhem, is poetry because it is the perfection of statement. The Boston Hymn, the Concord Ode, and the other occasional pieces fall in another class, and do not seem to be important. The first two lines of the Ode,

> "O tenderly the haughty day
> Fills his blue urn with fire."

are for their extraordinary beauty worthy of some mythical Greek, some Simonides, some Sappho, but the rest of the lines are commonplace. Throughout his poems there are good bits, happy and golden lines, snatches of grace. He himself knew the quality of his poetry, and wrote of it,

> "All were sifted through and through,
> Five lines lasted sound and true."

He is never merely conventional, and his poetry, like his prose, is homespun and sound. But his ear was defective: his rhymes are crude, and his verse is often lame and unmusical, a fault which can be countervailed by nothing but force, and force he lacks. To say that his ear was defective is hardly strong enough. Passages are not uncommon which hurt the reader and unfit him to proceed; as, for example:—

> "Thorough a thousand voices
> Spoke the universal dame:
> 'Who telleth one of my meanings
> Is master of all I am.'"

He himself has very well described the impression his verse is apt to make on a new reader when he says,—

> "Poetry must not freeze, but flow."

The lovers of Emerson's poems freely acknowledge all these defects, but find in them another element, very subtle and rare, very refined and elusive, if not altogether unique. This is the mystical element or strain which qualifies many of his poems, and to which some of them are wholly devoted.

There has been so much discussion as to Emerson's relation to the mystics that it is well here to turn aside for a moment and consider the matter by itself. The elusiveness of "mysticism" arises out of the fact that it is not a creed, but a state of mind. It is formulated into no dogmas, but, in so far as it is communicable, it is conveyed, or sought to be conveyed, by symbols. These symbols to a sceptical or an unsympathetic person will say nothing, but the presumption among those who are inclined towards the cult is that if these symbols convey anything at all, that thing is mysticism. The mystics are right. The familiar phrases, terms, and symbols of mysticism are not meaningless, and a glance at them shows that they do tend to express and evoke a somewhat definite psychic condition.

There is a certain mood of mind experienced by most of us in which we feel the mystery of existence; in which our consciousness seems to become suddenly separated from our thoughts, and we find ourselves asking, "Who am I? What are these thoughts?" The mood is very apt to overtake us while engaged in the commonest acts. In health it is always momentary, and seems to coincide with the instant of the transition and shift of our attention from one thing to another. It is probably connected with the transfer of energy from one set of faculties to another set, which occurs, for instance, on our waking from sleep, on our hearing a bell at night, on our observing any common object, a chair or a pitcher, at a time when our mind is or has just been thoroughly preoccupied with something else. This displacement of the attention occurs in its most notable form when we walk from the study into the open fields. Nature then attacks us on all sides at once, overwhelms, drowns, and destroys our old thoughts, stimulates vaguely and all at once a thousand new ideas, dissipates all focus of thought and dissolves our attention. If we happen to be mentally fatigued, and we take a walk in the country, a sense of immense relief, of rest and joy, which nothing else on earth can give, accompanies this distraction of the mind from its problems. The reaction fills us with a sense of mystery and expansion. It brings us to the threshold of those spiritual experiences which are the obscure core and reality of our existence, ever alive within us, but generally veiled and subconscious. It brings us, as it were, into the ante-chamber of art, poetry, and music. The condition is one of excitation and receptiveness, where art may speak and we shall understand. On the other hand, the condition shows a certain dethronement of the will and attention which may ally it to the hypnotic state.

Certain kinds of poetry imitate this method of nature by calling on us with a thousand voices at once. Poetry deals often with vague or contradictory statements, with a jumble of images, a throng of impressions. But in true poetry the psychology of real life is closely followed. The mysticism is momentary. We are not kept suspended in a limbo, "trembling like a guilty thing surprised," but are ushered into another world of thought and feeling. On the other hand, a mere statement of inconceivable things is the *reductio ad absurdum* of poetry, because such a statement puzzles the mind, scatters the attention, and does to a certain extent superinduce the "blank misgivings" of mysticism. It does this, however, *without* going further and filling the mind with new life. If I bid a man follow my reasoning closely, and then say, "I am the slayer and the slain, I am the doubter and the doubt," I puzzle his mind, and may succeed in reawakening in him the sense he has often had come over him that we are ignorant of our own destinies and cannot grasp the meaning of life. If I do this, nothing can be a more legitimate opening for a poem, for it is an opening of the reader's mind. Emerson, like many other highly organized persons, was acquainted with the mystic mood. It was not momentary with him. It haunted him, and he seems to have believed that the whole of poetry and religion was contained in the mood. And no one can gainsay that this mental condition is intimately connected with our highest feelings and leads directly into them.

The fault with Emerson is that he stops in the ante-chamber of poetry. He is content if he has brought us to the hypnotic point. His prologue and overture are excellent, but where is the argument? Where is the substantial artistic content that shall feed our souls?

The Sphinx is a fair example of an Emerson poem. The opening verses are musical, though they are handicapped by a reminiscence of the German way of writing. In the succeeding verses we are lapped into a charming reverie, and then at the end suddenly jolted by the question, "What is it all about?" In this poem we see expanded into four or five pages of verse an experience which in real life endures an eighth of a second, and when we come to the end of the mood we are at the end of the poem.

There is no question that the power to throw your sitter into a receptive mood by a pass or two which shall give you his virgin attention is necessary to any artist. Nobody has the knack of this more strongly than Emerson in his prose writings. By a phrase or a common remark he creates an ideal atmosphere in which his thought has the directness of great poetry. But he cannot do it in verse. He seeks in his verse to do the very thing which he avoids doing in his prose: follow a logical method. He seems to know too much what he is about, and to be content with doing too little. His mystical poems, from the point of view of such criticism as this, are all alike in that they all seek to do the same thing. Nor does he always succeed. How does he sometimes fail in verse to say what he conveys with such everlasting happiness in prose!

> "I am owner of the sphere,
> Of the seven stars and the solar year,
> Of Caesar's hand and Plato's brain,
> Of Lord Christ's heart and Shakespeare's strain."

In these lines we have the same thought which appears a few

pages later in prose: "All that Shakespeare says of the king, yonder slip of a boy that reads in the corner feels to be true of himself." He has failed in the verse because he has thrown a mystical gloss over a thought which was stronger in its simplicity; because in the verse he states an abstraction instead of giving an instance. The same failure follows him sometimes in prose when he is too conscious of his machinery.

Emerson knew that the sense of mystery accompanies the shift of an absorbed attention to some object which brings the mind back to the present. "There are times when the cawing of a crow, a weed, a snowflake, a boy's willow whistle, or a farmer planting in his field is more suggestive to the mind than the Yosemite gorge or the Vatican would be in another hour. In like mood, an old verse, or certain words, gleam with rare significance." At the close of his essay on History he is trying to make us feel that all history, in so far as we can know it, is within ourselves, and is in a certain sense autobiography. He is speaking of the Romans, and he suddenly pretends to see a lizard on the wall, and proceeds to wonder what the lizard has to do with the Romans. For this he has been quite properly laughed at by Dr. Holmes, because he has resorted to an artifice and has failed to create an illusion. Indeed, Dr. Holmes is somewhere so irreverent as to remark that a gill of alcohol will bring on a psychical state very similar to that suggested by Emerson; and Dr. Holmes is accurately happy in his jest, because alcohol does dislocate the attention in a thoroughly mystical manner.

There is throughout Emerson's poetry, as throughout all of the New England poetry, too much thought, too much argument. Some of his verse gives the reader a very curious and subtle impression that the lines are a translation. This is because he is closely following a thesis. Indeed, the lines are a translation. They were thought first, and poetry afterwards. Read off his poetry, and you see through the scheme of it at once. Read his prose, and you will be put to it to make out the connection of ideas. The reason is that in the poetry the sequence is intellectual, in the prose the sequence is emotional. It is no mere epigram to say that his poetry is governed by the ordinary laws of prose writing, and his prose by the laws of poetry.

The lines entitled Days have a dramatic vigor, a mystery, and a music all their own:—

> "Daughters of Time, the hypocritic Days,
> Muffled and dumb like barefoot dervishes,
> And marching single in an endless file,
> Bring diadems and fagots in their hands.
> To each they offer gifts after his will,
> Bread, kingdoms, stars, and sky that holds them all.
> I, in my pleached garden, watched the pomp,
> Forgot my morning wishes, hastily
> Took a few herbs and apples, and the Day
> Turned and departed silent. I, too late,
> Under her solemn fillet saw the scorn."

The prose version of these lines, which in this case is inferior, is to be found in Works and Days: "He only is rich who owns the day.... They come and go like muffled and veiled figures, sent from a distant friendly party; but they say nothing, and if we do not use the gifts they bring, they carry them as silently away."

That Emerson had within him the soul of a poet no one will question, but his poems are expressed in prose forms. There are passages in his early addresses which can be matched in English only by bits from Sir Thomas Browne or Milton, or from the great poets. Heine might have written the following parable into verse, but it could not have been finer. It comes from the very bottom of Emerson's nature. It is his uttermost. Infancy and manhood and old age, the first and the last of him, speak in it.

"Every god is there sitting in his sphere. The young mortal enters the hall of the firmament; there is he alone with them alone, they pouring on him benedictions and gifts, and beckoning him up to their thrones. On the instant, and incessantly, fall snowstorms of illusions. He fancies himself in a vast crowd which sways this way and that, and whose movements and doings he must obey; he fancies himself poor, orphaned, insignificant. The mad crowd drives hither and thither, now furiously commanding this thing to be done, now that. What is he that he should resist their will, and think or act for himself? Every moment new changes and new showers of deceptions to baffle and distract him. And when, by and by, for an instant, the air clears and the cloud lifts a little, there are the gods still sitting around him on their thrones,—they alone with him alone."

೧.

With the war closes the colonial period of our history, and with the end of the war begins our national life. Before that time it was not possible for any man to speak for the nation, however much he might long to, for there was no nation; there were only discordant provinces held together by the exercise on the part of each of a strong and conscientious will. It is too much to expect that national character shall be expressed before it is developed, or that the arts shall flourish during a period when everybody is preoccupied with the fear of revolution. The provincial note which runs through all our literature down to the war resulted in one sense from our dependence upon Europe. "All American manners, language, and writings," says Emerson, "are derivative. We do not write from facts, but we wish to state the facts after the English manner. It is the tax we pay for the splendid inheritance of English Literature." But in a deeper sense this very dependence upon Europe was due to our disunion among ourselves. The equivocal and unhappy self-assertive patriotism to which we were consigned by fate, and which made us perceive and resent the condescension of foreigners, was the logical outcome of our political situation.

The literature of the Northern States before the war, although full of talent, lacks body, lacks courage. It has not a full national tone. The South is not in it. New England's share in this literature is so large that small injustice will be done if we give her credit for all of it. She was the Academy of the land, and her scholars were our authors. The country at large has sometimes been annoyed at the self-consciousness of New England, at the atmosphere of clique, of mutual admiration, of isolation, in which all her scholars, except Emerson, have lived, and which notably enveloped the last little distinguished group of them. The circumstances which led to the isolation of Lowell, Holmes, Longfellow, and the Saturday Club fraternity are instructive. The ravages of the war carried off the poets, scholars, and philosophers of the generation which immediately followed these men, and by destroying their natural successors left them standing magnified beyond their natural size, like a grove of trees left by a fire. The war did more than kill off a generation of scholars who would have succeeded these older scholars. It emptied the universities by calling all the survivors into the field of practical life; and after the war ensued a period during which all the learning of the land was lodged in the heads of these older worthies who had made their mark long before. A certain complacency which piqued the country at large was seen in these men. An ante-bellum colonial posing, inevitable in their own day, survived with them. When Jared Sparks put Washington in the proper attitude for greatness by correcting his spelling, Sparks was in cue with the times. It was thought that a great man must have his hat handed to him by his biographer, and be ushered on with decency toward posterity. In the lives and letters of some of our recent public men there has been a reminiscence of this posing, which we condemn as absurd because we forget it is merely archaic. Provincial manners are always a little formal, and the pomposity of the colonial governor was never quite worked out of our literary men.

Let us not disparage the past. We are all grateful for the New England culture, and especially for the little group of men in Cambridge and Boston who did their best according to the light of their day. Their purpose and taste did all that high ideals and good taste can do, and no more eminent literati have lived during this century. They gave the country songs, narrative poems, odes, epigrams, essays, novels. They chose their models well, and drew their materials from decent and likely sources. They lived stainless lives, and died in their professors' chairs honored by all men. For achievements of this sort we need hardly use as strong language as Emerson does in describing contemporary literature: "It exhibits a vast carcass of tradition every year with as much solemnity as a new revelation."

The mass and volume of literature must always be traditional, and the secondary writers of the world do nevertheless perform a function of infinite consequence in the spread of thought. A very large amount of first-hand thinking is not comprehensible to the average man until it has been distilled and is fifty years old. The men who welcome new learning as it arrives are the picked men, the minor poets of the next age. To their own times these secondary men often seem great because they are recognized and understood at once. We know the disadvantage under which these Humanists of ours worked. The shadow of the time in which they wrote hangs over us still. The conservatism and timidity of our politics and of our literature to-day are due in part to that fearful pressure which for sixty years was never lifted from the souls of Americans. That conservatism and timidity may be seen in all our past. They are in the rhetoric of Webster and in the style of Hawthorne. They killed Poe. They created Bryant.

Since the close of our most blessed war, we have been left to face the problems of democracy, unhampered by the terrible complications of sectional strife. It has happened, however, that some of the tendencies of our commercial civilization go toward strengthening and riveting upon us the very traits encouraged by provincial disunion. Wendell Phillips, with a cool grasp of understanding for which he is not generally given credit, states the case as follows:—

"The general judgment is that the freest possible government produces the freest possible men and women, the most individual, the least servile to the judgment of others. But a moment's reflection will show any man that this is an unreasonable expectation, and that, on the contrary, entire equality and freedom in political forms almost invariably tend to make the individual subside into the mass and lose his identity in the general whole. Suppose we stood in England to-night. There is the nobility, and here is the church. There is the trading class, and here is the literary. A broad gulf separates the four; and provided a member of either can conciliate his own section, he can afford in a very large measure to despise the opinions of the other three. He has to some extent a refuge and a breakwater against the tyranny of what we call public opinion. But in a country like ours, of absolute democratic equality, public opinion is not only omnipotent, it is omnipresent. There is no refuge from its tyranny, there is no hiding from its reach; and the result is that if you take the old Greek lantern and go about to seek among a hundred, you will find not one single American who has not, or who does not fancy at least that he has, something to gain or lose in his ambition, his social life, or his business, from the good opinion and the votes of those around him. And the consequence is that instead of being a mass of individuals, each one fearlessly blurting out his own convictions, as a nation, compared to other nations, we are a mass of cowards. More than all other people, we are afraid of each other."

If we take a bird's-eye view of our history, we shall find that this constant element of democratic pressure has always been so strong a factor in moulding the character of our citizens, that there is less difference than we could wish to see between the types of citizenship produced before the war and after the war.

Charles Follen, that excellent and worthy German who came to this country while still a young man and who lived in the midst of the social and intellectual life of Boston, felt the want of intellectual freedom in the people about him. If one were obliged to describe the America of to-day in a single sentence, one could hardly do it better than by a sentence from a letter of Follen to Harriet Martineau written in 1837, after the appearance of one of her books: "You have pointed out the two most striking national characteristics, 'Deficiency of individual moral independence and extraordinary mutual respect and kindness.'"

Much of what Emerson wrote about the United States in 1850

is true of the United States to-day. It would be hard to find a civilized people who are more timid, more cowed in spirit, more illiberal, than we. It is easy to-day for the educated man who has read Bryce and Tocqueville to account for the mediocrity of American literature. The merit of Emerson was that he felt the atmospheric pressure without knowing its reason. He felt he was a cabined, cribbed, confined creature, although every man about him was celebrating Liberty and Democracy, and every day was Fourth of July. He taxes language to its limits in order to express his revolt. He says that no man should write except what he has discovered in the process of satisfying his own curiosity, and that every man will write well in proportion as he has contempt for the public.

Emerson seems really to have believed that if any man would only resolutely be himself, he would turn out to be as great as Shakespeare. He will not have it that anything of value can be monopolized. His review of the world, whether under the title of Manners, Self-Reliance, Fate, Experience, or what-not, leads him to the same thought. His conclusion is always the finding of eloquence, courage, art, intellect, in the breast of the humblest reader. He knows that we are full of genius and surrounded by genius, and that we have only to throw something off, not to acquire any new thing, in order to be bards, prophets, Napoleons, and Goethes. This belief is the secret of his stimulating power. It is this which gives his writings a radiance like that which shone from his personality.

The deep truth shadowed forth by Emerson when he said that "all the American geniuses lacked nerve and dagger" was illustrated by our best scholar. Lowell had the soul of the Yankee, but in his habits of writing he continued English tradition. His literary essays are full of charm. The Commemoration Ode is the high-water mark of the attempt to do the impossible. It is a fine thing, but it is imitative and secondary. It has paid the inheritance tax. Twice, however, at a crisis of pressure, Lowell assumed his real self under the guise of a pseudonym; and with his own hand he rescued a language, a type, a whole era of civilization from oblivion. Here gleams the dagger and here is Lowell revealed. His limitations as a poet, his too much wit, his too much morality, his mixture of shrewdness and religion, are seen to be the very elements of power. The novelty of the Biglow Papers is as wonderful as their world-old naturalness. They take rank with greatness, and they were the strongest political tracts of their time. They imitate nothing; they are real.

Emerson himself was the only man of his times who consistently and utterly expressed himself, never measuring himself for a moment with the ideals of others, never troubling himself for a moment with what literature was or how literature should be created. The other men of his epoch, and among whom he lived, believed that literature was a very desirable article, a thing you could create if you were only smart enough. But Emerson had no literary ambition. He cared nothing for belles-lettres. The consequence is that he stands above his age like a colossus. While he lived his figure could be seen from Europe towering like Atlas over the culture of the United States.

Great men are not always like wax which their age imprints. They are often the mere negation and opposite of their age. They give it the lie. They become by revolt the very essence of all the age is not, and that part of the spirit which is suppressed in ten thousand breasts gets lodged, isolated, and breaks into utterance in one. Through Emerson spoke the fractional spirits of a multitude. He had not time, he had not energy left over to understand himself; he was a mouthpiece.

If a soul be taken and crushed by democracy till it utter a cry, that cry will be Emerson. The region of thought he lived in, the figures of speech he uses, are of an intellectual plane so high that the circumstances which produced them may be forgotten; they are indifferent. The Constitution, Slavery, the War itself, are seen as mere circumstances. They did not confuse him while he lived; they are not necessary to support his work now that it is finished. Hence comes it that Emerson is one of the world's voices. He was heard afar off. His foreign influence might deserve a chapter by itself. Conservatism is not confined to this country. It is the very basis of all government. The bolts Emerson forged, his thought, his wit, his perception, are not provincial. They were found to carry inspiration to England and Germany. Many of the important men of the last half-century owe him a debt. It is not yet possible to give any account of his influence abroad, because the memoirs which will show it are only beginning to be published. We shall have them in due time; for Emerson was an outcome of the world's progress. His appearance marks the turning-point in the history of that enthusiasm for pure democracy which has tinged the political thought of the world for the past one hundred and fifty years. The youths of England and Germany may have been surprised at hearing from America a piercing voice of protest against the very influences which were crushing them at home. They could not realize that the chief difference between Europe and America is a difference in the rate of speed with which revolutions in thought are worked out.

While the radicals of Europe were revolting in 1848 against the abuses of a tyranny whose roots were in feudalism, Emerson, the great radical of America, the arch-radical of the world, was revolting against the evils whose roots were in universal suffrage. By showing the identify in essence of all tyranny, and by bringing back the attention of political thinkers to its starting-point, the value of human character, he has advanced the political thought of the world by one step. He has pointed out for us in this country to what end our efforts must be bent.

[1897]

Robert Browning

There is a period in the advance of any great man's influence between the moment when he appears and the moment when he has become historical, during which it is difficult to give any succinct account of him. We are ourselves a part of the thing we would describe. The element which we attempt to isolate for purposes of study is still living within us. Our science becomes tinged with autobiography. Such must be the fate of any essay on Browning written at the present time.

The generation to whom his works were unmeaning has hardly passed away. The generation he spoke for still lives. His influence seems still to be expanding. The literature of Browning dictionaries, phrase-books, treatises, and philosophical studies grows daily. Mr. Cooke in his Guide to Browning (1893) gives a condensed catalogue of the best books and essays on Browning, which covers many finely printed pages. This class of book—the text-book—is not the product of impulse. The text-book is a commercial article and follows the demand as closely as the reaper follows the crop. We can tell the acreage under cultivation by looking over the account books of the makers of farm implements. Thousands of people are now studying Browning, following in his footsteps, reading lives of his heroes, and hunting up the subjects he treated.

This Browningism which we are disposed to laugh at is a most interesting secondary outcome of his influence. It has its roots in natural piety, and the educational value of it is very great. Browning's individuality created for him a personal following, and he was able to respond to the call to leadership. Unlike Carlyle, he had something to give his disciples beside the immediate satisfaction of a spiritual need. He gave them not only meal but seed. In this he was like Emerson; but Emerson's little store of finest grain is of a different soil. Emerson lived in a cottage and saw the stars over his head through his skylight. Browning, on the other hand, loved pictures, places, music, men and women, and his works are like the house of a rich man,—a treasury of plunder from many provinces and many ages, whose manners and passions are vividly recalled to us. In Emerson's house there was not a peg to hang a note upon,—"this is his bookshelf, this his bed." But Browning's palace craves a catalogue. And a proper catalogue to such a palace becomes a liberal education.

Robert Browning was a strong, glowing, whole-souled human being, who enjoyed life more intensely than any Englishman since Walter Scott. He was born among books; and circumstances enabled him to follow his inclinations and become a writer,—a poet by profession. He was, from early youth to venerable age, a centre of bounding vitality, the very embodiment of spontaneous life; and the forms of poetry in which he so fully and so accurately expressed himself enable us to know him well. Indeed, only great poets are known so intimately as we know Robert Browning.

Religion was at the basis of his character, and it was the function of religious poetry that his work fulfilled. Inasmuch as no man invents his own theology, but takes it from the current world and moulds it to his needs, it was inevitable that Robert Browning should find and seize upon as his own all that was optimistic in Christian theology. Everything that was hopeful his spirit accepted; everything that was sunny and joyful and good for the brave soul he embraced. What was distressing, he rejected or explained away. In the world of Robert Browning *everything* was right.

The range of subject covered by his poems is wider than that of any other poet that ever lived; but the range of his ideas is exceedingly small. We need not apologize for treating Browning as a theologian and a doctor of philosophy, for he spent a long life in trying to show that a poet is always really both—and he has almost convinced us. The expositors and writers of textbooks have had no difficulty in formulating his theology, for it is of the simplest kind; and his views on morality and art are logically a part of it. The "message" which poets are conventionally presumed to deliver, was, in Browning's case, a very definite creed, which may be found fully set forth in any one of twenty poems. Every line of his poetry is logically dedicated to it.

He believes that the development of the individual soul is the main end of existence. The strain and stress of life are incidental to growth, and therefore desirable. Development and growth mean a closer union with God. In fact, God is of not so much importance in Himself, but as the end towards which man tends. That irreverent person who said that Browning uses "God" as a pigment made an accurate criticism of his theology. In Browning, God is adjective to man. Browning believes that all conventional morality must be reviewed from the standpoint of how conduct affects the actor himself, and what effect it has on his individual growth. The province of art and of all thinking and working is to make these truths clear and to grapple with the problems they give rise to.

The first two fundamental beliefs of Browning—namely: (1) that, ultimately speaking, the most important matter in the world is the soul of a man; and (2) that a sense of effort is coincident with development—are probably true. We instinctively feel them to be true, and they seem to be receiving support from those quarters of research to which we look for light, however dim. In the application of his dogmas to specific cases in the field of ethics, Browning often reaches conclusions which are fair subjects for disagreement. Since most of our conventional morality is framed to repress the individual, he finds himself at war with it—in revolt against it. He is habitually pitted against it, and thus acquires modes of thought which sometimes lead him into paradox—at least, to conclusions at odds with his premises. It is in the course of exposition, and incidentally to his main purpose as a teacher of a few fundamental ideas, that Browning has created his masterpieces of poetry.

Never was there a man who in the course of a long life changed less. What as a boy he dreamed of doing, that he did. The thoughts of his earliest poems are the thoughts of his latest. His tales, his songs, his monologues, his dramas, his jests, his sermons, his rage, his prayer, are all upon the same theme: whatever fed his mind nourished these beliefs. His interest in the world was solely an interest in them. He saw them in history and in music; his travels and studies brought him back nothing else but proofs of them; the universe in each of its manifestations was a commentary upon them. His nature was the simplest, the most positive, the least given to abstract speculation, which England can show in his time. He was not a thinker, for he was never in doubt. He had recourse to disputation as a means of inculcating truth, but he used it like a lawyer arguing a case. His conclusions are fixed from the start. Standing, from his infancy, upon a faith as absolute as that of a martyr, he has never for one instant undergone the experience of doubt, and only knows that there is such a thing because he has met with it in other people. The force of his feelings is so much greater than his intellect that his mind serves his soul like a valet. Out of the whole cosmos he takes what belongs to him and sustains him, leaving the rest, or not noting it.

There never was a great poet whose scope was so definite. That is the reason why the world is so cleanly divided into people who do and who do not care for Browning. One real glimpse into him gives you the whole of him. The public which loves him is made up of people who have been through certain spiritual experiences to which he is the antidote. The public which loves him not consists of people who have escaped these experiences. To some he is a strong, rare, and precious elixir, which nothing else will replace. To others, who do not need him, he is a boisterous and eccentric person,—a Heracles in the house of mourning.

Let us remember his main belief,—the value of the individual. The needs of society constantly require that the individual be suppressed. They hold him down and punish him at every point. The tyranny of order and organization—of monarch or public opinion—weights him and presses him down. This is the inevitable tendency of all stable social arrangements. Now and again there arises some strong nature that revolts against the influence of conformity which is becoming intolerable,—against the atmosphere of caste or theory; of Egyptian priest or Manchester economist; of absolutism or of democracy.

And this strong nature cries out that the souls of men are being injured, and that they are important; that your soul and my soul are more important than Caesar—or than the survival of the fittest. Such a voice was the voice of Christ, and the lesser saviors of the world bring always a like message of revolt: they arise to fulfil the same fundamental need of the world.

Carlyle, Emerson, Victor Hugo, Browning, were prophets to a generation oppressed in spirit, whose education had oppressed them with a Jewish law of Adam Smith and Jeremy Bentham and Malthus, of Clarkson and Cobden,—of thought for the million, and for man in the aggregate. "To what end is all this beneficence, all this conscience, all this theory?" some one at length cries out. "For whom is it in the last analysis that you legislate? You talk of *man*, I see only *men*."

To men suffering from an age of devotion to humanity came Robert Browning as a liberator. Like Carlyle, he was understood first in this country because we had begun earlier with our theoretical and practical philanthropies, and had taken them more seriously. We had suffered more. We needed to be told that it was right to love, hate, and be angry, to sin and repent. It was a revelation to us to think that we had some inheritance in the joys and passions of mankind. We needed to be told these things as a tired child needs to be comforted. Browning gave them to us in the form of a religion. There was no one else sane or deep or wise or strong enough to know what we lacked.

If ever a generation had need of a poet,—of some one to tell them they might cry and not be ashamed, rejoice and not find the reason in John Stuart Mill; some one who should justify the claims of the spirit which was starving on the religion of humanity,—it was the generation for whom Browning wrote.

Carlyle had seized upon the French Revolution, which served his ends because it was filled with striking, with powerful, with grotesque examples of individual force. In his Hero Worship he gives his countrymen a philosophy of history based on nothing but worship of the individual. Browning with the same end in view gave us pictures of the fifteenth and sixteenth centuries in France and Italy. He glorified what we had thought crime and error, and made men of us. He was the apostle to the educated of a most complex period, but such as he was, he was complete. Those people to whom he has been a poet know what it is for the heart to receive full expression from the lips of another.

The second thesis which Browning insists on—the identity of spiritual suffering with spiritual growth—is the one balm of the world. It is said that recent physiological experiment shows that muscles do not develop unless exercised up to what is called the "distress point." If this shall prove to be an instance of a general law,—if the struggles and agony of the spirit are really signs of an increase of that spiritual life which is the only sort of life we can conceive of now or hereafter,—then the truth-to-feeling of much of Browning's poetry has a scientific basis. It cannot be denied that Browning held firmly two of the most moving and far-reaching ideas of the world, and he expanded them in the root, leaf, flower, and fruit of a whole world of poetic disquisition.

It is unnecessary at this day to point out the beauties of Browning or the sagacity with which he chose his effects. He gives us the sallow wife of James Lee, whose soul is known to him, Pippa the silk-spinning girl, two men found in the morgue, persons lost, forgotten, or misunderstood. He searches the world till he finds the man whom everybody will concur in despising, the mediaeval grammarian, and he writes to him the most powerful ode in English, the mightiest tribute ever paid to a man. His culture and his learning are all subdued to what he works in; they are all in harness to draw his thought. He mines in antiquity or drags his net over German philosophy or modern drawing-rooms,—all to the same end.

In that miracle of power and beauty—The Flight of the Duchess—he has improvised a whole civilization in order to make the setting of contrast which shall cause the soul of the little duchess to shine clearly. In Childe Roland he creates a cycle, an epoch of romance and mysticism, because he requires it as a stage property. In A Death in the Desert you have the East in the first century—so vividly given that you wish instantly to travel there, Bible in hand, to feel the atmosphere with which your Bible ought always to have been filled. His reading brings him to Euripides. He sees that Alcestis can be set to his theme; and with a week or two of labor, while staying in a country house, he draws out of the Greek fable the world of his own meaning and shows it shining forth in a living picture of the Greek theatre which has no counterpart for vitality in any modern tongue.

The descriptive and narrative powers of Browning are above, beyond, and outside of all that has been done in English in our time, as the odd moments prove which he gave to the Pied Piper, The Ride from Ghent to Aix, Incident in the French Camp. These chips from his workshop passed instantly into popular favor because they were written in familiar forms.

How powerfully his gifts of utterance were brought to bear upon the souls of men will be recorded, even if never understood, by literary historians. It is idle to look to the present generation for an intelligible account of One Word More, Rabbi Ben Ezra, Prospice, Saul, The Blot on the 'Scutcheon. They must be judged by the future and by men who can speak of them with a steady lip.

It must be conceded that the conventional judgments of society are sometimes right, and Browning's mission led him occasionally into paradox and *jeux d'esprit*. Bishop Blougram is an attempt to discover whether a good case cannot be made out for the individual hypocrite. The Statue and the Bust is frankly a *reductio ad absurdum*, and ends with a query.

There is more serious trouble with others. The Grammarian's Funeral is false to fact, and will appear so to posterity. The grammarian was not a hero, and our calmer moments show us that the poem is not a great ode. It gave certain people the glow of a great truth, but it remains a paradox and a piece of exaggeration. The same must be said of a large part of Browning. The New Testament is full of such paradoxes of exaggeration, like the parable of the unjust steward, the rich man's chance for heaven, the wedding garment; but in these, the truth is apparent,— we are not betrayed. In Browning's paradoxes we are often led on and involved in an emotion over some situation which does not honestly call for the emotion.

The most noble quality in Browning is his temper. He does not proceed, as liberators generally do, by railing and pulling down. He builds up; he is positive, not negative. He is less bitter than Christianity itself.

While there is no more doubt as to the permanent value of the content of Browning than of the value of the spiritual truths of the New Testament, there is very little likelihood that his poems will be understood in the remote future. At present, they are following the waves of influence of the education which they correct. They are built like Palladio's Theatre at Vincenza, where the perspective converges toward a single seat. In order to be subject to the illusion, the spectator must occupy the duke's place. The colors are dropping from the poems already. The feeblest of them lose it first. There was a steady falling off in power accompanied by a constant increase in his peculiarities during the last twenty years of his life, and we may make some surmise as to how Balaustion's Adventure will strike posterity by reading Parleyings with Certain People.

The distinctions between Browning's characters—which to us are so vivid—will to others seem less so. Paracelsus and Rabbi

Ben Ezra, Lippo Lippi, Karshish, Caponsacchi, and Ferishtah will all appear to be run in the same mould. They will seem to be the thinnest disguises which a poet ever assumed. The lack of the dramatic element in Browning—a lack which is concealed from us by our intense sympathy for him and by his fondness for the trappings of the drama—will be apparent to the after-comers. They will say that all the characters in The Blot on the 'Scutcheon take essentially the same view of the catastrophe of the play; that Pippa and Pompilia and Phene are the same person in the same state of mind. In fact, the family likeness is great. They will say that the philosophic monologues are repetitions of each other. It cannot be denied that there is much repetition,— much threshing out of old straw. Those who have read Browning for years and are used to the monologues are better pleased to find the old ideas than new ones, which they could not understand so readily. When the later Browning takes us on one of those long afternoon rambles through his mind,—over moor and fen, through jungle, down precipice, past cataract,—we know just where we are coming out in the end. We know the place better than he did himself. Nor will posterity like Browning's manners,—the dig in the ribs, the personal application, and *de te fabula* of most of his talking. These unpleasant things are part of his success with us to whom he means life, not art. Posterity will want only art. We needed doctrine. If he had not preached, we would not have listened to him. But posterity evades the preachers and accepts only singers. Posterity is so dainty that it lives on nothing but choice morsels. It will cull such out of the body of Browning as the anthologists are beginning to do already, and will leave the great mass of him to be rediscovered from time to time by belated sufferers from the philosophy of the nineteenth century.

⁂

There is a class of persons who claim for Browning that his verse is really good verse, and that he was a master of euphony. This cannot be admitted except as to particular instances in which his success is due to his conformity to law, not to his violation of it.

The rules of verse in English are merely a body of custom which has grown up unconsciously, and most of which rests upon some simple requirement of the ear.

In speaking of the power of poetry we are dealing with what is essentially a mystery, the outcome of infinitely subtle, numerous, and complex forces.

The rhythm of versification seems to serve the purpose of a prompter. It lets us know in advance just what syllables are to receive the emphasis which shall make the sense clear. There are many lines in poetry which become obscure the instant they are written in prose, and probably the advantages of poetry over prose, or, to express it modestly, the excuse for poetry at all, is that the form facilitates the comprehension of the matter. Rhyme is itself an indication that a turning-point has been reached. It punctuates and sets off the sense, and relieves our attention from the strain of suspended interest. All of the artifices of poetical form seem designed to a like end. Naturalness of speech is somewhat sacrificed, but we gain by the sacrifice a certain uniformity of speech which rests and exhilarates. We need not, for the present, examine the question of euphony any further, nor ask whether euphony be not a positive element in verse,—an element which belongs to music.

The negative advantages of poetry over prose are probably sufficient to account for most of its power. A few more considerations of the same negative nature, and which affect the vividness of either prose or verse, may be touched upon by way of preface to the inquiry, why Browning is hard to understand and why his verse is bad.

Every one is more at ease in his mind when he reads a language which observes the ordinary rules of grammar, proceeds by means of sentences having subjects and predicates, and of which the adjectives and adverbs fall easily into place. A doubt about the grammar is a doubt about the sense. And this is so true that sometimes when our fears are allayed by faultless grammar we may read absolute nonsense with satisfaction. We sometimes hear it stated as a bitter epigram, that poetry is likely to endure just in proportion as the form of it is superior to the content. As to the "inferiority" of the content, a moment's reflection shows that the ideas and feelings which prevail from age to age, and in which we may expect posterity to delight, are in their nature, and of necessity, commonplace. And if by "superiority of form" it is meant that these ideas shall be conveyed in flowing metres,—in words which are easy to pronounce, put together according to the rules of grammar, and largely drawn from the vulgar tongue,—we need not wonder that posterity should enjoy it. In fact, it is just such verse as this which survives from age to age.

Browning possesses one superlative excellence, and it is upon this that he relies. It is upon this that he has emerged and attacked the heart of man. It is upon this that he may possibly fight his way down to posterity and live like a fire forever in the bosom of mankind.

His language is the language of common speech; his force, the immediate force of life. His language makes no compromises of any sort. It is not subdued to form. The emphasis demanded by the sense is very often not the emphasis demanded by the metre. He cuts his words and forces them ruthlessly into lines as a giant might force his limbs into the armor of a mortal. The joints and members of the speech fall in the wrong places and have no relation to the joints and members of the metre.

He writes like a lion devouring an antelope. He rends his subject, breaks its bones, and tears out the heart of it. He is not made more, but less, comprehensible by the verse-forms in which he writes. The sign-posts of the metre lead us astray. He would be easier to understand if his poems were printed in the form of prose. That is the reason why Browning becomes easy when read aloud; for in reading aloud we give the emphasis of speech, and throw over all effort to follow the emphasis of the metre. This is also the reason why Browning is so unquotable—why he has made so little effect upon the language—why so few of the phrases and turns of thought and metaphor with which poets enrich a language have been thrown into English by him. Let a man who does not read poetry take up a volume of Familiar Quotations, and he will find page after page of lines and phrases which he knows by heart—from Tennyson, Milton, Wordsworth—things made familiar to him not by the poets, but by the men whom the poets educated, and who adopted their speech. Of Browning he will know not a word. And yet Browning's poetry is full of words that glow and smite, and which have been burnt into and struck into the most influential minds of the last fifty years.

But Browning's phrases are almost impossible to remember, because they are speech not reduced to poetry. They do not sing, they do not carry. They have no artificial buoys to float them in our memories.

It follows from this uncompromising nature of Browning that when, by the grace of inspiration, the accents of his speech do fall into rhythm, his words will have unimaginable sweetness. The music is so much a part of the words—so truly spontaneous—that other verse seems tame and manufactured beside his.

Rhyme is generally so used by Browning as not to subserve the true function of rhyme. It is forced into a sort of superficial conformity, but marks no epoch in the verse. The clusters of rhymes are clusters only to the eye and not to the ear. The necessity of rhyming leads Browning into inversions,—into expansions of sentences beyond the natural close of the form,—into every sort of contortion. The rhymes clog and distress the sentences.

As to grammar, Browning is negligent. Some of his most eloquent and wonderful passages have no grammar whatever. In Sordello grammar does not exist; and the want of it, the strain upon the mind caused by an effort to make coherent sentences out of a fleeting, ever-changing, iridescent maze of talk, wearies and exasperates the reader. Of course no one but a school-master desires that poetry shall be capable of being parsed; but every one has a right to expect that he shall be left without a sense of grammatical deficiency.

The Invocation in The Ring and the Book is one of the most beautiful openings that can be imagined.

"O lyric love, half angel and half bird,
And all a wonder and a wild desire—
Boldest of hearts that ever braved the sun,
Took sanctuary within the holier blue,
And sang a kindred soul out to his face—
Yet human at the red-ripe of the heart—
When the first summons from the darkling earth
Reached thee amid thy chambers, blanched their blue,
And bared them of the glory—to drop down,
To toil for man, to suffer or to die—
This is the same voice: can thy soul know change?
Hail then, and hearken from the realms of help!
Never may I commence my song, my due
To God who best taught song by gift of thee,
Except with bent head and beseeching hand—
That still, despite the distance and the dark
What was, again may be; some interchange
Of grace, some splendor once thy very thought,
Some benediction anciently thy smile;—
Never conclude, but raising hand and head
Thither where eyes, that cannot reach, yet yearn
For all hope, all sustainment, all reward,
Their utmost up and on—so blessing back
In those thy realms of help, that heaven thy home,
Some whiteness, which, I judge, thy face makes proud,
Some wanness where, I think, thy foot may fall."

These sublime lines are marred by apparent grammatical obscurity. The face of beauty is marred when one of the eyes seems sightless. We re-read the lines to see if we are mistaken. If they were in a foreign language, we should say we did not fully understand them.

In the dramatic monologues, as, for instance, in The Ring and the Book and in the innumerable other narratives and contemplations where a single speaker holds forth, we are especially called upon to forget grammar. The speaker relates and reflects,—

pours out his ideas in the order in which they occur to him,—pursues two or three trains of thought at the same time, claims every license which either poetry or conversation could accord him. The effect of this method is so startling, that when we are vigorous enough to follow the sense, we forgive all faults of metre and grammar, and feel that this natural Niagara of speech is the only way for the turbulent mind of man to get complete utterance. We forget that it is possible for the same thing to be done, and yet to be subdued, and stilled, and charmed into music.

Prospero is as natural and as individual as Bishop Blougram. His grammar is as incomplete, yet we do not note it. He talks to himself, to Miranda, to Ariel, all at once, weaving all together his passions, his philosophy, his narrative, and his commands. His reflections are as profuse and as metaphysical as anything in Browning, and yet all is clear,—all is so managed that it lends magic. The characteristic and unfathomable significance of this particular character Prospero comes out of it.

> "*Prospero.* My brother and thy uncle, called Antonio—
> I pray thee mark me,—that a brother should
> Be so perfidious!—he whom next thyself,
> Of all the world I lov'd, and to him put
> The manage of my state; as at that time
> Through all the seignories it was the first,
> And Prospero, the Prime Duke, being so reputed
> In dignity and for the liberal arts,
> Without a parallel: those being all my study,
> The government I cast upon my brother,
> And to my state grew stranger, being transported
> And wrapped in secret studies. Thy false uncle—
> Dost thou attend me?"

It is unnecessary to give examples from Browning of defective verse, of passages which cannot be understood, which cannot be construed, which cannot be parodied, and which can scarcely be pronounced. They are mentioned only as throwing light on Browning's cast of mind and methods of work. His inability to recast and correct his work cost the world a master. He seems to have been condemned to create at white heat and to stand before the astonishing draft, which his energy had flung out, powerless to complete it.

We have a few examples of things which came forth perfect, but many of even the most beautiful and most original of the shorter poems are marred by some blotches that hurt us and which one feels might have been struck out or corrected in half an hour. How many of the poems are too long! It is not that Browning went on writing after he had completed his thought,— for the burst of beauty is as likely to come at the end as at the beginning,—but that his thought had to unwind itself like web from a spider. He could not command it. He could only unwind and unwind.

Pan and Luna is a sketch, as luminous as a Correggio, but not finished. Caliban upon Setebos, on the other hand, shows creative genius, beyond all modern reach, but flounders and drags on too long. In the poems which he revised, as, for instance, Hervé Riel, which exists in two or more forms, the corrections are verbal, and were evidently done with the same fierce haste with which the poems were written.

We must not for an instant imagine that Browning was indolent or indifferent; it is known that he was a taskmaster to himself. But he *could* not write other than he did. When the music came and the verse caught the flame, and his words became sweeter, and his thought clearer, then he could sweep down like an archangel bringing new strains of beauty to the earth. But the occasions when he did this are a handful of passages in a body of writing as large as the Bible.

Just as Browning could not stop, so he found it hard to begin. His way of beginning is to seize the end of the thread just where he can, and write down the first sentence.

> "She should never have looked at me,
> If she meant I should not love her!"

> "Water your damned flowerpots, do—"

"No! for I'll save it! Seven years since."

"But give them me, the mouth, the eyes, the brow!"

"Fear Death? to feel the fog in my throat."

Sometimes his verse fell into coils as it came, but he himself, as he wrote the first line of a poem, never knew in what form of verse the poem would come forth. Hence the novel figures and strange counterpoint. Having evolved the first group of lines at haphazard, he will sometimes repeat the form (a very complex form, perhaps, which, in order to have any organic effect, would have to be tuned to the ear most nicely), and repeat it clumsily. Individual taste must be judge of his success in these experiments. Sometimes the ear is worried by an attempt to trace the logic of the rhymes which are concealed by the rough jolting of the metre. Sometimes he makes no attempt to repeat the first verse, but continues in irregular improvisation.

Browning never really stoops to literature; he makes perfunctory obeisance to it. The truth is that Browning is expressed by his defects. He would not be Robert Browning without them. In the technical part of his art, as well as in his spirit, Browning represents a reaction of a violent sort. He was too great an artist not to feel that his violations of form helped him. The blemishes in The Grammarian's Funeral—*hoti's business, the enclitic de*—were stimulants; they heightened his effects. They helped him make clear his meaning, that life is greater than art. These savageries spoke to the hearts of men tired of smoothness and platitude, and who were relieved by just such a breaking up of the ice. Men loved Browning not only for what he was, but also for what he was not.

These blemishes were, under the circumstances, and for a limited audience, strokes of art. It is not to be pretended that, even from this point of view, they were always successful, only that they are organic. The nineteenth century would have to be lived over again to wipe these passages out of Browning's poetry.

In that century he stands as one of the great men of England. His doctrines are the mere effulgence of his personality. He himself was the truth which he taught. His life was the life of one of his own heroes; and in the close of his life—by a coincidence which is not sad, but full of meaning—may be seen one of those apparent paradoxes in which he himself delighted.

Through youth and manhood Browning rose like a planet calmly following the laws of his own being. From time to time he put forth his volumes which the world did not understand. Neglect caused him to suffer, but not to change. It was not until his work was all but finished, not till after the publication of The Ring and the Book, that complete recognition came to him. It was given him by men and women who had been in the nursery when he began writing, who had passed their youth with his minor poems, and who understood him.

In later life Browning's powers declined. The torrent of feeling could no longer float the raft of doctrine, as it had done so lightly and for so long. His poems, always difficult, grew dry as well.

But Browning was true to himself. He had all his life loved converse with men and women, and still enjoyed it. He wrote constantly and to his uttermost. It was not for him to know that his work was done. He wrote on manfully to the end, showing, occasionally, his old power, and always his old spirit. And on his death-bed it was not only his doctrine, but his life that blazed out in the words:—

> "One who never turned his back, but marched breast forward,
> Never doubted clouds would break,
> Never dreamed, though right were worsted, wrong would triumph.
> Held, we fall to rise—are baffled to fight better—Sleep to wake."

[1898]

Unpublished Correspondence

To his wife Minna Timmins Chapman

Feb. 10, 1892

... Read *The Scarlet Letter*. It is a very strong book, if not a great book, and has a great hold on life. Little Pearl is the weakness of it—and she is superfluous. A phantastic child is a disagreeable object. The charm of children is to be like other children. The things the child says and does and her double entendres are strained and manufactured, and laid on too heavy—one might have been permitted as an accident. The book is to my mind a very wonderful work of art. Painful in the extreme but full of truth. Hester Prynne doesn't impress me as a real character—rather a fine abstraction of a woman, but the two men—Chillingworth and Dimmesdale—are masterpieces. The time occupied in the development of the plot is false to nature—seven years. The reactions would have taken place inside twelve months. Human beings do not lie at that pace for seven years.

Neither would Dimmesdale have died in that appropriate manner—he would have recovered. Hawthorne knew this perfectly well, but he considered his death absolutely necessary for the tragic note. I cannot imagine a man who should have acted as Dimmesdale did at the beginning nor imagine that he should not have been suspected from the start. Flirtations require time and place in this world, and upon this fact rests the safety of social institutions.

To Minna Timmins Chapman

Thursday—Sept. 8, 1892

Amor mio

I finished Arnold's *Life of Lincoln*. It is a wonderful story very well told. I wish you would read it. You must know the history of the world pretty accurately before you can realize how rare a man Lincoln was. It is the added margin of forbearance—the wisdom of the future—the point of view of the future and the large horizon. These he never lost—never lost his head. But he could have done nothing without the people. On the continent of Europe he would have been misunderstood and shovelled aside as an enthusiast. None other than the American people would have reelected him.

And you cannot read the history of the Civil War without marvelling at the people as much as at Lincoln. His shrewdness, his mysticism, his humor, his humanity were all recognized and understood and backed up—in an extraordinary and intimate way. Had he been eccentric in these qualities, he would have been useless. I cannot be sorry he died when he did. Whatever service he could have done by however long a life—supposing him to have escaped the pitfalls of mistake, unpopularity he would have been sure to fall into, nothing could have so served his country as his taking off almost like Elijah—which makes his life seem like a miracle play. The country was revealed by him to itself—and his sudden death typified, made sacred, what he did and was. It has done more to unify the country than any one thing. It has set a frame about him like a holy picture. The shock of it has made Americans of us all. Time cannot touch him. He is protected. The study of his record shows him daily greater. What was best of him—what he could do at his uttermost, that he did. That remains. No new or greater course for him is imaginable. And to have this immortal part of him lifted up—treasured and enshrined forever by his death—this was his greatest fortune. It is his greatest gift to his country.

To Martin Brimmer

March 21, 1893

My dear Mr. Brimmer

... We have reached a period of comparative calm on the amusement side of life. Went last night to hear Jo Jefferson lecture on the drama—which meant—make an after-dinner, rambling lot of remarks excellently delivered, but not up to concert pitch, and as he was in a great concert hall we were disappointed. He's a very charming person and said to be very ready—tho' this was a prepared speech and he is actually popular, and yet there is something about the loose-jointed, old-fashioned, ante-bellum Americanism which he represents, that I don't think as good as it's cracked up to be. His manner of speaking and of telling his stories was perfect.

It was a subscription performance for the benefit of kindergartens. Gilder, the editor of the *Century*, is the president of the association and thrust himself forward to make some foolish remarks in an artificial voice—Gilder ought to be suppressed. He is small and quiet-looking, but he is as numerous as the Australian rabbit. Go out to dinner—Gilder, open a magazine—Gilder, speak of a charity—Gilder again, poetry—Gilder, the new school of acting—Gilder, oratory—Gilder. He don't bestride the world like a colossus, but he pervades the world like grasshoppers and sparrows, and since he has adopted this artificial voice and taken to speaking in public, life in New York has become intolerable. We are therefore going to stay at home tonight and exclude the periodicals—even the evening papers.

To Mrs. Henry Whitman

327 West Eighty-Second Street
[1893]

My dear Mrs. Whitman

Minna called at the Bourgets today—just received your note as carriage drove up to the door—also asked 'em to dine Saturday when by chance we were giving a dinner party—so you see your letter was well timed. I am against Bourget. I don't care how charming he is. His photographs are posé. I intend to be rude and queer to him. I'm glad he talks English as my most limited French prevents all nuances of hostility and enforces a sort of meaningless politeness—like that of a deaf person. As for his parched books—some of them dried by gas light and cigarettes and all of them choking and this last phase of his—high art, morality, sentimentality, religiosity—the most hopeless of all symptoms. This is the sort of impression I intend *not to change about him*.

Yours affectionately
John Jay Chapman

There's a man in Chaucer—a very wicked man who said he was going to do the deed and *never would repent*.

To Mrs. Henry Whitman

[1893]

I forgot to abuse James Russell Lowell's letters of which I read a few in reviews, advance sheets, etc.—and won't read any more. I think they are self-conscious, literary, ointed, and twiddling, and the reverse of what letters ought to be. Good letters are violent—vivid, unconscious, rapid, colloquial—like Byron's, which are stunning—not that I like Byron, but he did know how to write manly and delightful letters. Parsonage puritan, Scarlet Letter parsonage, is what Minna says they are—so don't try to mitigate our aspersions—but suggest any book you come across. I have spoken too mildly of James Russell Lowell. I know from my constant admissions of the large excellence of this man and the generosity of my speech about him that you think I admire him. Indeed I do not. He is a cat to me. By the way, did you read the story of the Cat and the Cobra in the Evening Post last week or shall I send it to you? It is told with infinite appreciation of cats (I defer to you) and was very interesting. . . .

To Florence Lockwood

Venice
July 5, 1894

Dear Flos

Perfectly delighted at your engagement. Nothing has made me feel so young for years and years—as if things were happening, had happened, and about to happen. I wish I were nearer by to tell you so. I feel as if not only you but all of us had been moved back to the youth mark—and shown promised lands—and had wrinkles wiped out—and spoken to encouragingly by all creation. It gives me something to look forward to when I return alone two months hence to lead my Dantesque and solitary life. . . .

I can't go the Bellini craze—I understand how it arose—nor the Botticelli craze. The discovery of the merit of Botticelli & Co. happened to be coincident with a sentimental development of a highly objectionable kind. I don't doubt I should have shared it if I had been agoing—but it's thirty or forty years ago and passing rapidly. Mind, I don't deny the excellence of these fellows, the excellence of very similar fellows contemporary with them is so much beyond anything since that I can't believe my friends and the amateurs of today are led to admire these particular men except by the kaleidoscopic shifting of modern mode and sentiment which reveals from time to time some school or phase of art in the past and obscures others.

Carlo Dolce used to fill the sentimental bill as Botticelli does now. Botticelli is of course a much greater man and of the greatest time—but that's not [the] reason—nor the measure by which he is admired.

The trouble with all art is that no one is in a position to understand it who has not had a technical education in the branch you study—and nobody has that I know. Here's Burckhardt who writes on the Renaissance—can he draw a cow? Has he put up a shanty?—has he decorated anything? A country builder would probably be more fit to judge the real problem in the mind of the architect. Here's Ruskin who thinks Venice would have continued to rule the earth if she had only kept free from building the round gables. Burckhardt, the cleverest of them all and the most learned, can't see anything but contortions in Michael Angelo, and speaks of the soul in painting as if it were something distinct from the drawing, coloring, or whatnot of the physical properties of the canvas or paint. The painters, who ought to have some chance of knowing, are either ignorant or inarticulate. Have you seen the Della Robias in Venice in S. Giobbe? They were repairing them so we had a chance to see them near—on a chapel ceiling—mounted ladder to the top.

> Please remember me to
> LaFarge and believe me
> very affectionately
> John Jay Chapman

To Mrs. Henry Whitman

> 56 Wall Street
> Sept. 19, 1896

... In reading Emerson—and it's from reading Emerson for many years that I've got my habits of manner in writing—in reading Emerson—we get both precept and practice, in the form of freedom, freedom, freedom. But I have an aim above freedom and quite different. It is to express some particular idea or chain of thought. If the English of Charles Eliot Norton will do it or of Rossetti—I go for that English. Now I see from your note that somehow you do see *exactly* what I am trying to say about Browning—and you probably feel the same truths about the matter itself as strongly as I do—and so I wish you lived next door so that I could go over the thing for a week or two—because now I am convinced it is worth while. Last night as I was going to bed it seemed not worthwhile, for I thought the "Browningites won't like the essay because it is critical—and nobody else will *care about it anyway.*" The essay is a backbone merely—and the head, heart, hands, and feet, ribs, whiskers and watchchain I can always append to it in the shape of other essays.

For instance, I don't talk about "Love" in Browning—because it isn't a primary thing after all any more than it is in the world. There are other things to which we have to toe the mark.

J.J.C.

To Minna Timmins Chapman

Sept. 26, 1896

. . . It is easy to write smart things of Emerson in a private letter, but this is a question of values. I want to bring out some few traits—so that no one will think of questioning them and I think I see the way to do it. This is devilish personal work. It is like writing a poem. I am totally unworthy to come near Emerson from the point of view of character and shall miss his sublimity because I do not share it. You see also this—I have only got space about as large as this page in which to make clear the whole basis of transcendentalism—fortunately it is a simple thing. My seven years' sojourn in New England, the fact that I am really of New England stock and sympathize with them, the fact that I grew up as a child in a different climate and have lived in a different climate since, gives me great advantages. I understand them—but they do not understand me.

It is curious, but Emerson's books seem so small a part of the element I really am trying to grasp. He is a Dial. What an excellent name for a paper that was—the best name a newspaper ever had. . . .

To his future wife Elizabeth Chanler

July 6, 1897

... Lord forgive me Elizabeth—I must tell you what goes through my mind—however unjust or improper to say. Sometimes I'm jealous of you as if you had compartments in your mind labeled "other people's business" that I must not share. There's no such compartment. I haven't the smallest curiosity about other people's business—but you mustn't have any such idea in your head—no division—no compartment. Why Elizabeth you're all mine and I yours completely. I know no such distinction in my mind. I turn it all over just as it stands—and you must do the same. No other people will be damaged. Don't be afraid. But both you and I will be damaged by any such notion. It's the notion I object to. That's not marriage. That's friendship or something else. So burn up that notion. It will evaporate of itself—be absorbed, like the tendons they tie up wounds with, into our one flesh and blood. Nothing could keep it alive. It will merge and melt—but I only tell you and prophesy this beforehand. If such pocketing *were* going to damage, hurt, injure anyone else—I'd say let them be hurt. Let them be consumed—Elizabeth and I are one flesh and mind. My mind is her mind. This is and is to be. If this hurts let them perish, for it cannot be stayed nor hindered. Don't oppose me nor set up individualistic theories or diplomacy or moral notions nor loyalty notions nor other people's business notions. All things that ever were told to you from the beginning of time was told with the promise and distinct understanding that as between you and me was to be no privacy—no wall no retention. No other thing than this is the union—or the understanding of it among all tribes—nations—polities—where monogamy prevails. There darling—I haven't one single thing—instance, matter, or thought in my mind as to anything I want to know about—nor do I have any expectation of having any—but only on the general idea of things between us.

At the bottom of all is a greater matter—that only in the sharing of thought lies truth. All things are half things—dead or crooked till looked at with the beloved, so that it were truer to say that all these things were half lights—till now only given this—penumbra—never seen in their true relations nor with health. There darling I hope you understand, for if you don't it makes no difference—for you will act so and feel so and indeed you do now.

To Elizabeth Chanler

July 27, 1897

... Tell you a secret. It don't make any difference what subject you write on. The subject is the thread the crystals form on. It's an incident. Montaigne never had any subject. Emerson never had any subject. The value of anything is not because it's about some subject—but because somebody thinks it. The writer's mind is the only subject. The only unity is the organic unity of all coming from one place. Suppose I did write what satisfied Mrs. Crafts—it could only be because the stuff was sawed into *her* lengths. It's almost a necessity that a new creature—for I swear that I am a new creature—I swear any man who will write his own thoughts—is a new creature—should shock, should antagonize, should startle.

To Elizabeth Chanler

New York
Feb. 5, 1898

... Holden tells me if I were thorough I would go into a cell and be a mystic—prophesies I will be a Roman Catholic—I told him all right, let it come. Who's afraid? Told me I must know George Searles, a Paulist father—talked about St. Paul, Francis of Assisi, and Buddhism. The cell business is on his brain. He tries to show me all my reforms, etc. are rot. Incidentally, to illustrate the use of a cell in inducing the religious point of view and spiritual life shutting off sensations, he spoke of Baron Trenck, Casanova, etc. "But," I said—"You have protected me—I won't *go* near a cell—for fear of becoming a saint. Count me out. I'm a politician, and now I see how to stay a politician." Then he went on illogically—to say he'd just written an article absolutely proving that the doctrine that "A man *was* what his occupation made him" was not true in the Cosmopolitan. He regards the thing as a dangerous error. I say ain't that extraordinary, and ain't it pathetic? N.B. He himself is some sort of a Buddhist—Easternism of some sort. Easternism plays the deuce with the Western nature. He says he is not a Roman Catholic. He says I'm a mass of intellectual pride—but that my intellectual honesty will bring me out a mystic. I said, "Fire away!"

I never knew a clearer case of convictions being the outcome of occupation—astronomy—Eastern thought—political corruption—personal honesty and despair will make Holden. He's a great believer in a future life. I rather think this belief is a danger. It makes people lazy. I have never thought about the matter myself and never intend to think about it. I'm sure that if there be a future life I'm on the right track to reach it—it may turn out that I've always believed in it. I do doubt the existence of the external world—and shouldn't be surprised to wake up any time and find it all a mirage. I am so fixed and positive in this doubt that I don't see how anyone else can feel in any other way about the matter. The result of this talk with Holden was to make me long for Wall Street as the only road to heaven—to you—to love—to Christ.

I say who can say that we haven't got the beginnings of civilization in America—when I find a man talking like this on 43rd St. There you have a true curiosity about life—which is the beginning of all things....

To Elizabeth Chanler Chapman

Munich
Ap. 23, 1908

... Read a long life of Schumann from which one couldn't learn as much about him as from two bars of his music. The book is all taken up with psychological analysis—the most inexpressive of all forms of human activity. Schumann is rather an obscure person—so great and yet always a little off—a little out of focus—except in the songs. And I'm not sure that a lyric isn't permitted to be a little overstrained by its nature—a little sick, lovesick, or homesick. But I don't feel quite at home in Schumann—though I admire him as much as anyone can, both for his character, his writing and his music: and the whole course of his life.

His literary and philosophic interests—his earliest passions were literary passions—seem to have got between him and his music. The very second-rate German poetry and philosophy—Jean Paul—Fichte—and whatnot were his earliest interests. If he had only never learned how to read. His music is all a little cloudy and impure—muddled. It is the devil for a musician to bother with metaphysics—except musical metaphysics. If he is a musician first, last, and all the time, it is no harm for him to read. He sees only music. But at the time Schumann ought to have been learning counterpoint he was pretending to study law and was really reading metaphysical novels and writing illustrative music. See the depth to which Bach or Beethoven were always immersed in the material they worked in. "It should go thus—that theme," says Bach on hearing some[one] play the beginning of a fugue, "ought to take such and such a course—now let us see how he manages." They are the slaves of the material. All this which you and I call technique is merely honesty—honest subjection.

You know Schumann wanted to express something. All the same he's a much greater man than Mendelssohn who was the very picture of true musical training. . . .

To his mother, Eleanor Jay Chapman

Badminton
Glos. England
May 23, 1908

. . . Elizabeth is paying a round of visits—with friends. I begged off, owing to my Paris experiences, and I dare say she will have a better sort of time without me, as they are old friends and she'll have them more to herself. Besides I'm not very safe and the English are rather down in the mouth and very sensitive. I got through all right with the few people I saw at Oxford one afternoon. But if I had met them again next day I feel sure I should have educated them, and I don't want to.

A strange thing has happened in England—everyone is polite. It's very noticeable and almost uncanny. I don't like it. The people you meet in the cars make meeching remarks in praise of U.S.A. Most insincere and pitiable. They are the least downright people on the globe. They have swagger or servility, but nothing between. I don't want to see them at all just now—as I myself am too apt to go loose and ramp up and down. I almost did it after James's lecture—when shaking hands with a few old harmless people. It would have been disgusting. At Oxford you have the acme of luxury and dumb-headed cant.

Why, Boston isn't in it for complacency, and their culture is pretty trivial. It's all sort of a varnish for politics. I saw a subject for a prize essay on a bulletin board—"Compare the British Empire with other Empires past and present." Imagine a boy who should make any comparison to the disadvantage of the B.E.—would he get a prize? I never before understood the desire to destroy a stained glass window till I attended some of their luxurious services—pomp and emptiness. It's mere decoration now. This is not a very good spirit to visit Oxford in. It's not what is expected—and it's not quite fair. . . .

To Eleanor Jay Chapman

Parker House
Boston
July 25: 1909

My dear Mama

No. I will not apologize: but I will explain.

I know that you have not the least idea of what sort of letters you write. But what happens is something like this—You sit down to write when you are irritated. Perhaps a cabman has overcharged you; perhaps you are not feeling well because you sat in a draft the evening before. Very well. You begin a note to me and you empty out all your ill humor (perhaps just and righteous ill humor towards somebody else) *on me*. You are so unconscious of what you are doing that you are surprised and hurt to find that your letter has not been a pleasant, agreeable letter to receive. Really, I have done nothing to make me the object of such abusive letters, complaining about the house and everything in it as you have been writing to me. It's most unjust and wrong that you should write me such letters. There's nothing remarkable about that house, or about the fact that you should be living in it. It's no special subject for gratitude on your part. It's a natural situation. I don't want gratitude. I only want you not to use the house as an excuse for writing long, hacking, discontented diatribes to me.

Well: you don't know what your letters are like. It occurred to me that I should write you a letter just in the same spirit as yours to me, that is to say—expressing my exact state of mind when in a state of irritation. That is what my letter to you does. Now you know how it feels to get a letter written in order to work off irritation. I got rid of that irritation by writing that letter. I worked off that irritation on you. But mind you, it was your irritation to begin with. I only just sent it back to you in the same package.

There may be something morally wrong about this. Perhaps I should accept your letters and try to soothe you and sympathize—or perhaps I rather think I should just burn them and try to think of something else, when they are rasping epistles. Well, I generally do this. But this last time I didn't.

That is all.

Yours affly
Jack

To William James

Camden, Me.
Sept. 2: 1909

My dear James

My deep personal interest in you survives the shock of the books and articles you write. Like the bower anchor it rides the waves—high-hearted triumphant. But whether it can outlive your "Mrs. Piper's Hodgson control"—(the by-products of your muse) I don't know. "Time was that when the brains were out the man would die," but now—

Just saw Miss Agnes Irwin at lunch at the Shattucks. I'd like to have a talk with her about the inward rottenness of Harvard College. She *looks* as if she knew.

Yours
J.J.C.

To Elizabeth Chanler Chapman

Train to Boston
Feb. 19, 1910

... There is a town on this railroad called New Haven, at which the train stops for five minutes. It is an unconscionable time to stop—because there's really nothing there, you know, and no reason why they should stop at all. After standing it as long as I could, I whiled away the time by buying some sandwiches, which had a taste like oleomargarine mixed with wagon-grease. This comes of taking these vulgar trains. The 1 o'clock doesn't make one think of such things.

On the 1 o'clock train you are free from all the habitués and local people who go to these queer little places along the road. I confess it disturbs me to see vulgar people. I find myself wondering what they do and where they live and whether they *feel* vulgar, and whether it would do any good to tell them how vulgar and useless they are, how much better I should be without them. I feel this desire to educate them and lift them up; but then it is so annoying to be always doing good to others. Why shouldn't somebody come along sometime and do me good? That's what I want to know....

To William Rothenstein

Barrytown-on-Hudson
October 20th, 1912

My dear Rothenstein

... Some day about fifty years hence I am coming over to England to make an inquest in the wake of W. Rothenstein and find out what genius, or schools of decoration, or ethics, or poetry, have sprung up, evoked by your *affetuoso guido*. For I believe there will be response; though in what *form* it is yet too soon to say. Certainly one must wait a generation longer in your case than in that of the ordinary man; for you are somehow a *precursor*—(you're the only one I've ever seen—and I didn't know that genius existed till I saw you.) This doesn't preclude your being a painter—on the contrary, it's more apt to follow from it—but it's a separate function. I am disappointed that the artists I know won't paint what I want them to and in *my way*, but they don't seem to. I see so many landscapes, for instance, about here, that seem to cry out to be painted; I see such pretty children in the cottages—I swear I could almost paint them myself. But the painters whom I know are interested in stunts, virtuosity, and processes. The truth is that it is so difficult to paint at all—that when a man thinks he sees how to do some corner of it, he's very likely to spend his whole life over the problem.

Yours sincerely
J.J.C.

To Elizabeth Chanler Chapman

325 W 82
Nov. 20, [1913]

... *The Magic Flute* was beyond all expectation beautiful. I'd ever so much rather hear it than Kreisler—who is all over in a minute. It gave me a new conception of Mozart. So far as sound goes

Mozart is the greatest musician that ever lived. Bach and Beethoven are greater men—and had greater ideas—but they are not in it with Mozart in the use of either voices or instruments—or in an understanding of how to do things that *sound well* with the scale and with harmony. To take an extreme case—a Beethoven quartette *sounds* very often like the devil. The instrumentation of Mozart is the most wonderful thing ever done on the earth, I think. Beethoven's symphonies are handsome things—but they are like sawing wood (in this particular respect) compared to Mozart.

The orchestra was amazingly well played—one never heard such an orchestra in opera—never abroad—and perhaps this is why I was so struck. . . .

The following letter concerns the second edition of the recipient's *Ancient Ideals: A Study of Intellectual and Spiritual Growth from Early Times to the Establishment of Christianity* (1896), which appeared in 1913.

To Henry Osborn Taylor

325 W. 82
Dec. 31, 1913

Dear Harry

I have been reading *Ancient Ideals*—a most valuable sort of book, just the kind I can read. I only like school books and I remain always in the fifth form. I confess to reading even this kind of book with the utmost doubt and cynicism. The chapter on the early Greeks seems to have stood through the Cretan discoveries, and is most admirable in its brevity. As for the bursts of lyric about the Greeks, and Life with a large L and all that, damned if the Greeks seem like that to me. That part seems a little old-fashioned. Have the chapter on Greek philosophy still to read. I approach it with loathing. Have you ever read Montaigne's Essay XII—the long one (originally the introduction to his translation of Sebond, done at his father's request when he was a young man)? It is the strongest thing in literature, and disposes of the Greek world so far as philosophy goes—to my mind, anyway. It is at the bottom of Shakespeare's conception of Hamlet. As for the candied buncombe of Pericles' speeches, which have been the prolegomena of the 19th century view of the Greeks, you might as well take Edward Everett's speeches on our Revolutionary fathers as a view of America. The difference is only *in form*. They played up every weakness of the Athenian and caused her downfall. Truly viewed, they show up the Greeks. It gives me labor pains and strange inward vomits to read them.

Yours
J.J.C.

Bibliography

Primary Sources

The Two Philosophers: A Quaint and Sad Comedy. Boston: J. G. Cupples Company, 1892.
Causes and Consequences. New York: Charles Scribner's Sons, 1898. Reprint. New York: Moffat, Yard and Company, 1909.
Emerson and Other Essays. New York: Charles Scribner's Sons, 1898. Reprint. New York: Moffat, Yard and Company, 1909.
Practical Agitation. New York: Charles Scribner's Sons, 1900. Reprint. New York: Moffat, Yard and Company, 1909.
Four Plays for Children. New York: Moffat, Yard and Company, 1908.
The Maid's Forgiveness: A Play. New York: Moffat, Yard and Company, 1908.
"The Harvard Classics and Harvard." *Science* 30 (1 Oct. 1909): 440–43.
A Sausage from Bologna: A Comedy in Four Acts. New York: Moffat, Yard and Company, 1909.
Learning and Other Essays. New York: Moffat, Yard and Company, 1910.
The Treason and Death of Benedict Arnold: A Play for a Greek Theatre. New York: Moffat, Yard and Company, 1910.

Neptune's Isle and Other Plays for Children. New York: Moffat, Yard and Company, 1911.
William Lloyd Garrison. New York: Moffat, Yard and Company, 1913. Reprint. Boston: Atlantic Monthly Press, 1921.
Deutschland über Alles; or, Germany Speaks. New York: G. P. Putnam's Sons, 1914.
Homeric Scenes: Hector's Farewell and the Wrath of Achilles. New York: Laurence J. Gomme, 1914.
Greek Genius and Other Essays. New York: Moffat, Yard and Company, 1915.
Memories and Milestones. New York: Moffat, Yard and Company, 1915.
Notes on Religion. New York: Laurence J. Gomme, 1915.
Cupid and Psyche. New York: Laurence J. Gomme, 1916.
Victor Chapman's Letters from France, with Memoir by John Jay Chapman. New York: Macmillan Company, 1917.
Songs and Poems. New York: Charles Scribner's Sons, 1919.
A Glance toward Shakespeare. Boston: Atlantic Monthly Press, 1922.
Letters and Religion. Boston: Atlantic Monthly Press, 1924.
Dante. Boston: Houghton Mifflin Company, 1927.
Two Greek Plays: The Philoctetes of Sophocles and the Medea of Euripides. Boston: Houghton Mifflin Company, 1928.
The Antigone of Sophocles. Boston: Houghton Mifflin Company, 1930.
Lucian, Plato, and Greek Morals. Boston: Houghton Mifflin Company, 1931.
New Horizons in American Life. New York: Columbia University Press, 1932.
Retrospections. In *John Jay Chapman and His Letters* by M. A. DeWolfe Howe. Boston: Houghton Mifflin, 1937.
The Selected Writings of John Jay Chapman. Ed. Jacques Barzun. New York: Farrar, Straus, and Cudahy, 1957.
The Collected Works of John Jay Chapman. 12 vols. Ed. Melvin H. Bernstein. Bibliographical checklist by David M. Stocking. Weston, Mass.: M and S Press, 1970.
"Strongly-Flavored Imitation Cynicism." Review of Henry Adams's *Education.* Ed. Daniel Aaron. *New England Quarterly* 63 (June 1990): 288–93.

The Classical Writings of John Jay Chapman. Ed. William Arrowsmith. *Arion* 3d ser. 2.2 and 3 (Spring-Fall 1992–93).

Secondary Sources

Allen, Gay Wilson. "In Literature's Limbo." *Saturday Review*, 14 Nov. 1959, 29.

"An American Moralist." *Times Literary Supplement*, 14 Aug. 1930, 645–46.

Arvin, Newton. "A Mind That Was Spoken Freely." *New York Times Book Review*, 29 Sept. 1957.

Barzun, Jacques. "Against the Grain: John Jay Chapman." *Atlantic Monthly*, Feb. 1947, 120–24.

Bernstein, Melvin H. *John Jay Chapman.* New York: Twayne, 1964.

———. "John Jay Chapman and the Insurgent Individual." *American Radicals: Some Problems and Personalities.* New York: Monthly Review Press, 1957. 21–35.

Brown, Stuart Gerry. "John Jay Chapman and the Emersonian Gospel." *New England Quarterly* 25 (June 1952): 147–80.

Downey, Dennis B., and Raymond M. Hyser. *No Crooked Death: Coatesville, Pennsylvania, and the Lynching of Zachariah Walker.* Urbana: University of Illinois Press, 1991.

Fuller, Henry B. "Essays by John Jay Chapman." *New Republic*, 30 July 1924, 280.

Golder, Herbert S. "On First Looking into Arrowsmith's Chapman." *Arion* 3d ser. 2.2 and 3 (Spring-Fall 1992–93): 1–18.

Goldman, Eric F. "Summer Sunday." *American Heritage*, June 1964, 50–53.

Hovey, Richard B. *John Jay Chapman: An American Mind.* New York: Columbia University Press, 1959.

Howe, Helen. *The Gentle Americans, 1864–1960.* New York: Harper and Row, 1965.

Howe, M. A. DeWolfe. *John Jay Chapman and His Letters.* Boston: Houghton Mifflin, 1937.

Kazin, Alfred. "A Left-Over Transcendentalist." *New Republic*, 11 Nov. 1957, 16–18. Reprinted in *Contemporaries.* Boston: Little, Brown, 1962. 64–69.

Le Gallienne, Richard. "Dante as a Great Egoist." *New York Times Book Review*, 29 May 1927.

———. "John Jay Chapman on 'The Old Perfections of the Earth.'" *New York Times Book Review*, 15 June 1924, 5.

Loveman, Amy. "Fountain of Fire." *Saturday Review of Literature*, 9 Oct. 1937, 7.

Lynn, Kenneth S. "Chapman Still Challenges Us." *New York Herald Tribune Book Review*, 29 Sept. 1957.

———. "The Precepts of Emerson." *New York Times Book Review*, 29 Nov. 1959, 28.

McWilliams, Carey. "The Only True Defiance." *The Nation*, 13 Apr. 1970, 442–44.

Miller, Dickinson. "John Jay Chapman." *New Republic*, 20 Oct. 1937, 310.

Miller, Perry. "John Jay Chapman: A Meaning for Today." *Christian Science Monitor*, 26 Sept. 1957, 11.

O'Connor, W. V. "Emerson, Chapman, and Individualism." *Revue des Langues Vivantes* 21 (1955): 442–47.

Paul, Sherman. "The Identities of John Jay Chapman." *Journal of English and Germanic Philology* 59.2 (1960): 255–62.

Price, Lucien. "New Horizons in American Life." *New England Quarterly* 5 (Oct. 1932): 841–43.

Ricks, Christopher. "On Heroes and Anti-Hero-Worship." *Arion* 3 ser. 2.2 and 3 (Spring-Fall 1992–93): 19–26.

Rukeyser, Muriel. "Chapman." *A Turning Wind: Poems*. New York: Viking Press, 1939. 104–8.

Samuels, Ernest. "Rabid Idealist." *The Nation*, 5 Dec. 1959, 423–24.

Santayana, George. "The Alleged Catholic Danger." *New Republic*, 15 Jan. 1916, 269–71.

Sedgwick, Ellery. "*John Jay Chapman and His Letters*, by M. A. DeWolfe Howe." *Atlantic Monthly*, Dec. 1937.

Sherman, Stuart. "Essays of John Jay Chapman." *The Nation*, 7 Sept. 1911, 219–20. Reprinted in *Shaping Men and Women*. Garden City, N.Y.: Doubleday, Doran, 1928. 51–58.

[Stevens, Wallace?] "*Practical Agitation* by John Jay Chapman." *Harvard Advocate* 69 (10 May 1900): 80.

Stocking, David. "John Jay Chapman and Political Reform." *American Quarterly* 2 (Spring 1950): 62–70.

Van Doren, Mark. "Rich at Least." *The Nation*, 23 Oct. 1937, 440–

41. Reprinted in *The Private Reader.* New York: Henry Holt, 1942. 269–73.

Wellek, René. *American Criticism, 1900–1950.* Vol. 6 of *A History of Modern Criticism.* New Haven: Yale University Press, 1986.

Whicher, George F. "Trial and Error." *New York Herald Tribune Books,* 28 Aug. 1932, 10.

Wilson, Edmund. "John Jay Chapman." *New Republic,* 22 May 1929, 28–33.

———. "John Jay Chapman." *Atlantic Monthly,* Nov. 1937, 581–95. Reprinted in *The Triple Thinkers.* New York: Harcourt, Brace, 1938. Reprint. New York: Oxford University Press, 1948. 133–64.

———. *Letters on Literature and Politics.* Ed. Elena Wilson. New York: Farrar, Straus, and Giroux, 1977.

———. "Lucian versus Plato." *New Republic,* 30 Sept. 1931, 180–82.

———. "Mr. Chapman's Dante." *New Republic,* 18 May 1927, 361–63.

Wister, Owen. "John Jay Chapman." *Atlantic Monthly,* May 1934, 524–39.

———. "A Master Writer." *Yale Review* 11 (Apr. 1922): 629–32.

Richard Stone is a librarian who works as an assistant editor of *Book Review Digest*. In his spare time he collects and studies the writings of John Jay Chapman and other American thinkers.

Jacques Barzun, a translator, literary consultant, and author of more than two dozen books, has edited *The Selected Writings of John Jay Chapman*.